Alba Arikha was born and raised in Paris. She is the author of three other books: *Muse*, *W*[illegible] *Ice* and *Soon*. She has written for sever[illegible] teaches creative writing in Lond[illegible]th her husband and two [illegible]riter.

N[illegible]

'Alba Arikha has wr[illegible]onderfully atmospheric book. The story is a thrilling one – think *Schindler's List* but with extra twists and turns. On the one hand we are in Paris of the early eighties – riverside cafés, The Clash and first kisses. On the other, we are in eastern Europe in 1944, a place of trauma of the sort that takes generations to heal'

Mail on Sunday

'The ability to let prose ease into poetry, as Arikha does here, is rare'

Times Literary Supplement

'Anyone who's ever had a tantrum will recognise the helpless rage that comes with being 13, and her family's wartime experiences give Arikha's sparse prose a haunting melancholy'

Spectator

'The brevity of Alba Arikha's memoir belies its depth and breadth. It is a moving story of a young woman's coming of age and her father's struggle to overcome his horrific early experiences. Like Beckett, Alba makes every word count'

Jewish Chronicle

Other books by the author

Muse

Walking on Ice

Soon

MAJOR/MINOR

A Memoir

ALBA ARIKHA

QUARTET

Major / Minor was first published in 2011 by
Quartet Books Limited
A member of the Namara Group
27 Goodge Street, London W1T 2LD

This paperback edition published in 2017
by Quartet Books Limited

A catalogue record for this book
is available from the British Library

ISBN 978 0 7043 7433 1

Typeset by Antony Gray
Printed and bound in Great Britain by
T J International, Padstow

To my children, Ascanio and Arianna

In memory of my father,

Avigdor Arikha

1929–2010

How long ago the day is
when at last I look at it
with the time it has taken
to be there still in it

W. S. MERWIN

1

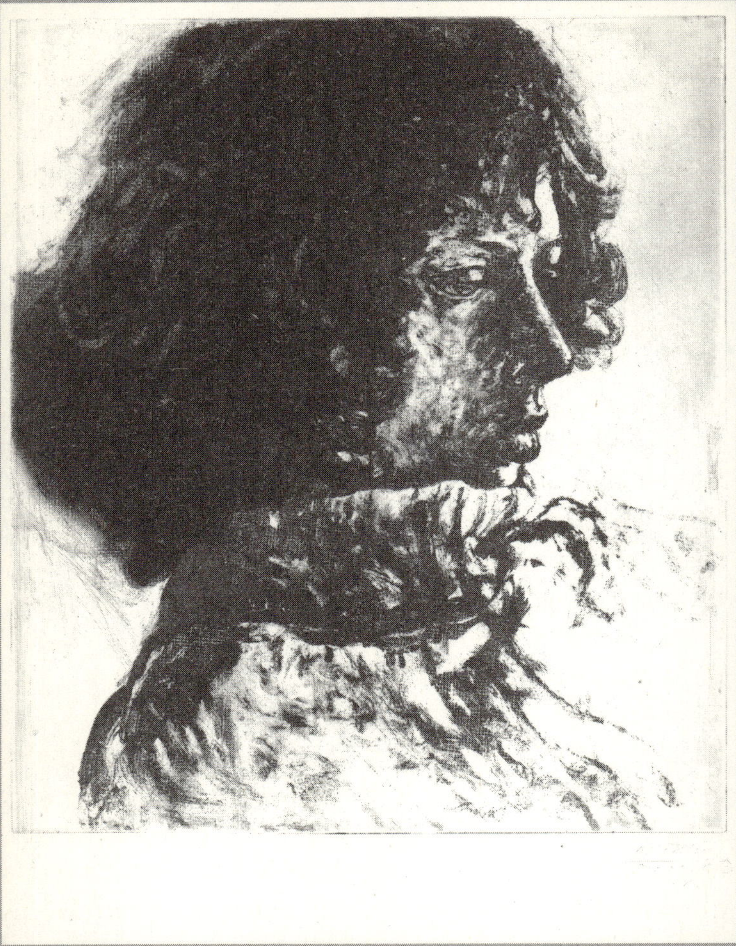

Pepi lives outside Jerusalem. The road leading up to her house smells of lavender and pine, mingled with manure from the nearby hills.

She is waiting for us on her doorstep, a small figure in a polka-dot dress. Her white, curly hair is soft like cotton, her caramel skin has the warmth of honey and sunshine. She hugs my father in German, kisses my mother in Hebrew, clasps my sister and me against her chest. When she releases her grasp, her soft brown eyes look at us attentively.

You are beautiful girls, she tells us.

Pepi speaks to us in French, which she learnt at school when she was a young girl. She rolls her r's with a gentle click of the tongue, and many of her sentences are grammatically incorrect. But we don't mind.

Liebe Kinder. Beautiful girls, she repeats wistfully.

Beautiful? No. Neither of us is beautiful. My sister hides beneath a mass of unruly curly hair and thick glasses. I walk straight and stiff, like a puppet on a string. A metal bar runs down my spine, a cotton scarf shielding the outside world from the sight of the ungainly pink contraption which begins underneath my chin and settles above my hips. Once we remove this back brace, you will look like a ballerina, the doctor had said.

Like a ballerina.

Anything but a ballerina.

Pepi's eyes fill with tears, as they do each time she sees us. Irrepressible tears which irritate me.
Why does she always cry? I ask my father.
Because she sees our existence as a miracle.
Why?
I already told you. During the war, we were destined to die, not to live.

This is a concept I cannot relate to. Life has barely begun, too soon for death even to enter the picture. My sister is nine years old, I am twelve. Soon, I will enter womanhood. I have nascent acne bumps to prove it. I will become beautiful and popular, and life will be good to me.
Life wasn't always good to my father, or to his mother, but now it is. One must move on, my father says. No need to dwell on the past.
Only his nocturnal screams are a reminder of what it was like: *Raus Jude! Achtung!* We can often hear him shout in his sleep. Nazi flashbacks, as my mother explains.

The power of my father's unconscious is startling. As if he mustn't be allowed to forget. I know about Nazis, about flashbacks. I know how embarrassed my father would be if he knew that we heard him.

I dread my own unconscious. I cannot think of anything worse than having my secrets exposed.

When I see my grandmother cry, I cringe. Same for my parents. A poem, a piece of music, a quote is enough to unleash in them a torrent of emotions which I find repellent. How could anyone let their emotions tumble out of their system like wet laundry? Where do their boundaries lie? I know about boundaries. I read about them in various books. Russian legends with swash-buckling soldiers and blushing maidens. French classics where bashfulness wins over brazenness. When naughty children overstep their boundaries they get punished, over and over again. I get reprimanded, but never punished. Anyway, it doesn't matter. I am as hard as steel, like the metal bar which holds my spine in place.

My sister, Noga, has skin like yogurt. Thick, white, creamy yogurt. Like me, she wears glasses with prescription lenses that dilate our eyes like bubbles, a device more suited to the elderly than the young girls that we are. But our vision needs to be corrected. This is not about how we look, says my father, but how we see. How the world sees us is irrelevant. One shouldn't care about what people think, we are told, over and over again. Don't you ever listen to anybody except yourself.

I listen to myself, but I also listen to my father.
And so does my grandmother. I see her face light up every time she looks at him and listens to his words. Vigo, she sighs. Lieber Vigo, she repeats, occasionally passing her hand through his curly hair. Her manicured nails are polished a deep red.

Why does she always say that? asks Noga. Why does she always repeat your name?

What do you expect after fourteen years of separation? answers my father.
Fourteen years of separation.

My mother asks us to follow Pepi inside the house. Her husband, Jean, gazes wearily at us. Thick lines cover his face like twigs and his hands tremble incessantly. He points his shaky finger towards a plate of biscuits. You like?
My sister shrugs her shoulders. Pepi walks over and admonishes Jean in German. He shakes his head slowly, like a tired dog.
Pepi disappears into the kitchen while my mother talks to Jean. Her voice sounds like a purr, and he listens with a large smile on his face. My father starts to pace around the room, nervously. Pepi emerges from the kitchen, holding a cake triumphantly. We sit around a table in her small garden, while she cuts the slices tenderly, as if she were caressing our cheeks. Eat, meine Kinder, eat.

We speak of my aunt, Elena, who lives in Jerusalem with her husband and two children. Elena is unwell, and Pepi worries about her. About her children, my cousins whom I barely know. My father disapproves of them. Of Elena's husband. Of Elena herself. She may have saved his life during the war, but she almost ruined it afterwards.
Do I need to remind you that she sold my drawings without telling me? That when I came back from my years in Paris to pick them up there was nothing left? NOTHING! All my drawings were gone. Everything. And all the money was spent, of course.

Pepi's eyes fill with tears again. She knows, Vigolein, she knows she did wrong. But that was thirty-five years ago. You must forgive her. She's ill. She has diabetes. She's unhappy.
Unhappy? I wonder why. And what did she do with your jewels? With your beautiful strand of pearls? Did she not sell that too, behind your back? Hmmm?
Stop it, my mother admonishes him. Stop it right now.

I can feel droplets of sweat gathering against my back like a nest of ants. My sister adjusts her glasses, places her hands on her knees and looks downwards.
The harsh Israeli sun, which gives no respite during the day, is starting to set. Soon it will be pitch dark. Sunsets don't linger here. Night-time happens quickly. A door slamming into darkness, black as coal.

2

Madame Balançoire wears the same blue and white dress every time I see her, in the Champ de Mars gardens.
She is the Queen of Swings. She sits behind her till, her hair pulled back in a strict bun. Occasionally a few strands come loose, especially at the end of the day.
When grown-ups are tired, they seem to crumple; things happen to their features. To their demeanour. To the sound of their voice.

The swing lady works hard, my father says.

Her work is my heaven.

The Queen hands out pink tickets to well-heeled mothers and docile children.
Pink tickets to the sky.
She smiles a lot and recognises us all. *Bonjour, ma puce. Ça va, mon ange? Oh, mais quelle jolie robe . . .*

I have just turned seven. For my birthday, my mother has invited fifteen children over to our apartment. We'll be playing American games, she announces.
We play pin the tail on the donkey, musical chairs and blind man's buff. We squeal with delight and gorge ourselves on sandwiches, ice cream and home-made chocolate cake. Secret recipe, I overhear her tell one of the mothers who sits in a corner, watching her child with a mindful eye.
(I like secrets.)
We sing French and English songs. When all the children have gone, I open my presents.
All mine.
No sharing.

The Queen of Swings leads my father and me towards one of the green, rusty swings. She helps me on, grabbing my hand.
Pousse tire, pousse tire, she says, giving the swing a vigorous push.
I tilt my head back, flying high towards the plane trees, their leaves rustling in the wind.
Towards the grey sky and the white clouds, soft like cotton candy.

Below me, I hear the sound of squealing children. Of a man laughing loudly. Of cars tearing down the streets. Of an aeroplane, in the distance.
The world is quiet up high. I close my eyes and glide, like a bird.
I forget about time and place.

Alba! Alba! You're going too high! You're going to fall!

I open my eyes and slow down.
I won't fall! I cry out. I'm holding on tight.
Enough! Time to go home.
One more turn, aba, please!
No. You've been on that swing long enough.
Please!

One more rip-roaring, swinging, lifting, tantalising feeling of freedom. Of utter glee.

Enough! my father repeats, sternly.

But I'm off anyway. Higher, and higher.
And then, back down.
Slowly, until my feet hit the firm ground.
Why didn't you listen to me? My father furrows his eyebrows, as he usually does when he reprimands me.
But I was having such fun . . .
He sighs, loudly. All right, all right.

Goodbye, Queen of Swings.

We walk towards the bus stop, past the École Militaire and the Avenue de Tourville, where we used to live. My father holds my hand, his warm and calloused skin against mine.
The Bells are coming to dinner, he says.
Will they bring me a present? I wonder. They often do.
The Bells have a country house in Saint-Paul de Vence. We visited them there, one summer. The garden smelled of pine and roses. There were blue shutters on the bedroom windows, which creaked at night. Noga was afraid; I wasn't.

Paul Bell is English. He prints art books and speaks in a booming voice. He is big and wears thick glasses which make his nose sweaty. His wife, Sylvie, has straight blonde hair and freckled skin. Her gums show when she smiles. They look red, like strawberries. When she drinks, Sylvie takes tiny sips and holds the liquid briefly in her mouth before swallowing it. Perhaps it's something to do with her gums.

3

Sometimes at night, when I cannot sleep, my father puts his hand on my back.
It is a soothing hand, filled with warmth and reassurance.
There, there, he says. Close your eyes and empty your thoughts.
It's too difficult to empty them, I say.
So I'll sing you a song, then. One my mother used to sing to me.
He begins to hum in German.
Eine alte Hexe um die Ecke.
Eine alte Hexe um die Ecke.

Then, this rhyme:
Eins zwei – Polizei – drei vier, Offizier – fünf sechs, alte Hex – sieben acht, gute Nacht – neun zehn, auf Wiedersehn

His words rock back and forth, like a cradle. He isn't singing but susurrating, his tongue clicking against his palate as the distant sounds of his childhood knock against mine.

After he leaves the room, I can still feel the heat of his palm against my skin.

4

At home, Kathleen runs us a bath.
Kathleen is our au pair from Texas. She is a tall brunette who washes her hair every day with an American shampoo. She always smells clean and her teeth are very white.
That's because she drank a lot of milk as a child, my mother says.
Kathleen's laugh is warm and infectious, just like her Southern twang. She's always in a good mood, even when my father roars; she isn't frightened of him because she understands him. She worked for a famous French actor before moving in with us. He was difficult too.

Often, Kathleen tells us stories about her home town and her boyfriend, Doug.
She carries Doug's picture in her wallet. He has dark hair, beady eyes and a moustache. I don't find him attractive.

Doug and I will be married one day, Kathleen says with a large smile on her face.
I think he looks like a fireman, I tell her.
Kathleen's smile has disappeared.
He's not a fireman, he's an insurance salesman, she says.
I like firemen, I say. They save people.
Well, in his own way, Doug saves people too, she answers.
She explains what insurance is. She speaks of deals and coverage. Of benefit and risk.

From what I can understand, the only risk to Kathleen is Doug.
But this time, I don't share my thought with her.

Kathleen studies cooking at Le Cordon Bleu school and practises at home: You'll be my guinea pigs, she says.
So we are.
She makes us Provençal dishes. Gourmet dishes. Simple country fare, which we eat heartily.
One evening, as we are devouring a roast chicken, Kathleen receives a phone call from Doug.
When she returns to the kitchen table, she is beaming.
Doug just asked me to marry him, she says. And I said yes. I'm flying back to Texas in two weeks. I'm really sorry, she adds, seeing the crestfallen looks on our faces.
We'll miss you, but I understand. Congratulations, my mother says, giving her a hug. I wish you much happiness with your fiancé.

The day of her departure, Kathleen kisses and hugs us tenderly.

I'll write and I want you to promise that you'll write back.
We nod in unison. We both feel like crying but hold our tears back.
Kathleen was a soothing presence in the house; my father was less angry when she was around. What will happen now?

Not much happens, we discover. Life is as it always was, minus Kathleen. Her features become indistinct in our minds, but not her smell: the shampoo bottle she left behind is a constant reminder of her presence. For months, that shampoo bottle will remain untouched on our bathtub, until my mother washes her hair with it one morning.
In order to keep her memory alive, I drink more milk after Kathleen's departure.
But my teeth will never look like hers.

5

The Louvre. I am nine years old, my sister is six. My father holds our hands while we skid on the shiny parquet floors.
Stop!
The Infanta Margarita. A pink ribbon in her hair, her black and white dress, her five-year-old eyes gazing at us from the canvas.
Stop again!
Mademoiselle Rivière. A beautiful young girl whom Ingres painted when she was fifteen years old, a year before she died. Her sleek brown hair is pulled back, revealing a long neck, blushed cheeks, full lips and porcelain skin. She wears a white dress and her gloved arm holds a white serpentine boa.

Mature beyond her years, there is something haunting about her. She could have been a wife. A lover. A mother. Or my friend, perhaps.

The landscape in the background was painted later, my father explains.
Indeed. There is something superficial about it, as if the picturesque panorama had been added to conceal the bleak demise of its young sitter.
One often died young in those days, I was told.
What if I were to die young? How many people would mourn me?

Last painting.
La Marquesa de la Solana by Goya. My sister and I are intimidated by her. Her pitch-black dress, her tall stature, her stern eyes.
But then, there are her shoes. Exquisitely small pumps underneath the heavy, imposing black taffeta dress.
Her small feet are her little secret.
We know her, I say.
My sister agrees. She's Dina.
My father laughs.
Enough. We've seen enough.
Never more than three or four paintings a day.

Dina is a wealthy patron of my father's work. She bought the flat we live in, originally purchased by another patron of my father's work. The flat is held in a family trust, and every visit by *le baron et la baronne*, dropped off by their faithful driver in a black Mercedes, entails a thorough cleaning-up and fussing about the place.

In essence, I know this. That my father has a great talent which cannot pay all our bills. So wealthy people who believe in him come to our rescue.

Nothing wrong with that. Talent is rare, money is rife.

Dina is tall and very thin, with equine nostrils and impeccably coiffed hair.

She lives in an *hôtel particulier* in the 16th arrondissement, with a garden the size of our local park. The daughter of a business magnate, the Canadian citizen married a French baron who smiles a lot and says little of consequence.

The couple live in utter luxury with their two sons, and are attended by a dizzying plethora of servants who wait on them around the clock. At lunchtime, we are served dishes in exquisite china. A servant clothed in a gold-buttoned white jacket, with matching white gloves, remains in the room with us. I often wonder whether he listens to our conversations and whether he actually cares. Needless to say, I will never know the answer. He remains as impassive as a Buckingham Palace guard, with not even a flicker of an emotion passing across his composed face.

Dina collects my father's paintings. With a keen eye for the arts and a sharp mind, she is revered around our household although I find her terrifying, and so does my sister. Perhaps it's her haughty manner. Or perhaps the mere fact that she is part of a world I do not understand.

6

There was a Dina in my mother's family. Savta's younger sister. She smoked long cigarettes and had a deep, husky voice, like the actress Simone Signoret. She lived alone in a small flat in Jerusalem.

There was something different about Dina. She wasn't religious, like the other members of her family. She was curious, and there was a quiet elegance about her. Although I barely knew her, when people asked me if I had family in Israel I often mentioned her. My great-aunt Dina, she's pretty cool, I would say casually.

What about your father's family?

Besides my grandmother, I don't really know them.

Why?

He has a sister he doesn't get along with, and he doesn't like her children. So we don't see them.

But they're your cousins!

We don't see them.

Don't you want to see them?

I shrug my shoulders. I cannot tell them that my father won't allow us to.

I don't really care, I mutter.

And that cousin you told me about?

Anna? She lives in Brazil.

Brazil? Cool.

Yes. But I don't know her. Although I heard that she might move to Paris.

You should get to know her.

Yes. I will.

II

My father and I walk into Pepi's living room and she greets us effusively.
Come in! Come in! she cries. She hugs me and holds me tightly against her. Her glasses make her eyes look smaller. When she kisses me, her face cream sticks to my cheek. Her skin looks smooth and tanned.
Pepi has baked a cake with white, fluffy icing on top. It sits on a circular wooden table, in the centre of the room. Around it, she has carefully placed white-lace napkins and small silver forks. I feel like dipping my finger into the surface of the icing and licking it off.
Pepi cuts us a slice and places it gently on a porcelain plate. Old recipe from Czernowitz, she tells my father. Do you remember it?
My father shakes his head. Maybe, I don't know, he answers. Sometimes he seems irritated with his mother, just as I am with mine. It's a strange comfort to me, although I suspect that my father fails to see the irony of it all.

We carry our plates to a worn sofa. Pepi sits down with some difficulty and pats a pillow. Sit here, she says.
I recline on her sofa and look out of the window. Two yellow plastic chairs stand on her terrace, by a small table. A green plant is inching through a pane of the French window.
The phone rings and Jean, wearing a bathrobe and slippers, picks it up slowly.

Hello, he says in a dreary voice.
He turns towards Pepi. It's Mrs Taubman, he says. About the cream.
Pepi pauses for a brief minute. Tell her I'll call her back, she says.

Jean relays the message in an equally monotone voice and hangs up. He then shuffles towards us and smiles timidly, adjusting the dressing-gown knot at his waist.
How's everything? he asks my father.
You tell me, my father says.
Jean shrugs his shoulders. Same old thing, he mutters. I'm going to change, he adds, before shuffling away in his noisy slippers.
I pick at my cake. How are you? Pepi asks me. How's school? Do you have many friends?
I shrug my shoulders. A few, here and there.
Do you like your school?
Yes. It's OK.

It's not OK. I want more friends and I hate school.
I also hate those polyester turtleneck sweaters my mother makes me wear in the winter.
And the long, flowing dresses she buys me every summer, which reveal the white, sebaceous bumps on my chest.
And the fact that no matter how hard I try to emulate the girls in my class, I always seem to be a step behind them.

Although I'd like to, I cannot share this information with Pepi; somehow, I don't think she'd understand. Why would she?

I think of Isabelle, a girl in my class. She often speaks of her grandmother, who has a big house in the Dordogne valley and who entertains writers and artists from all over the world.
She's great, Isabelle once said to me. We have a lot of fun together. She's full of energy, she swims every day and in the evening she loves a drink and a game of Scrabble.

Does Pepi drink? Does she play Scrabble?
Probably not. Pepi lives a world away from Isabelle's grandmother.
Whatever she may have suffered, Isabelle's grandmother overcame her pain, or at least pretended to the world that she had.
Pepi cannot pretend anything.
Her pain is an open window which has never been fully closed: she needs to grieve in order to feel alive.
The gulf between Pepi and me is insurmountable. However hard I try, I cannot get close to her. Only my father can reach her.
Or can he?

I think of Pepi as a younger woman.
Did she like to entertain? Did she know famous writers and artists? Does she even know how to swim?
Somehow, I imagine her as more constrained. A well-brought-up bourgeoise, who catered for her husband and children and forgot about herself somewhere along the line until she had only herself to cater for.

Why is it that one seeks to hide the truth from old people? Does

age diminish our ability to take in disheartening information? Perhaps I have it all wrong. Perhaps brittle bones do not equal brittle hearts.
I wish I could sit down with Pepi and tell her about my sorrows. But, in her case, it would be adding fuel to her frailty.

Pepi's living room smells mouldy, a bit like the German both she and my father are now speaking. I feel left out when they speak to each other. Why can't they include me? I'm twelve years old. Old enough to participate in conversation.
Or perhaps they're talking about me?
Pepi mentions David, her grandson. My father grumbles and Pepi seems upset.
She turns her face to look at me. Your father often gets upset, she says. He was always special that way.
I'm not sure why getting upset is so special, but I know that I want to go home. They should be alone, the two of them.
Pepi runs her long-nailed fingers through my curls and twists her fingers around them. What lovely hair you have, she says. She looks at my father. I wish Karl had known these girls. He would have been so proud.
Her eyes fill with tears again. Her pupils look watery behind her large-framed glasses.
My father looks uncomfortable. *Hör auf zu weinen,* he says. Stop crying.

But she doesn't.

There is something tragic about Pepi. The weight of her history sits between us insolubly; her present is so linked to her past that, no matter how light our banter, every word is a potential precipice.

I stand up quickly and wander about Pepi's living room. I give the objects which line the bookshelf a cursory glance: a photograph of Noga and me, as children. A few books, mostly in German and Romanian. A crystal vase. A large photograph of Tamar, Elena's daughter whom I barely know. She's my age, and lives somewhere outside Haifa. She has dark hair and a sad expression in her eyes. I spent an afternoon with her the previous summer. Her English was hesitant, as was her smile.

She's a nice girl, but look at the mother she has, my father remarked, after Elena had driven us home.

She's still your sister no matter what, my mother reminded him.

Look at what she's become, my father retorted. My opposite.

Is Tamar my opposite? Does it really matter if she is?

I pick up the photograph, searching for clues in her face. I drop it inadvertently. A loud noise ensues. What happened?

Nothing, nothing, I answer quickly, picking up the photograph and replacing it on the shelf.

Pepi gets up and disappears into her bedroom.

Why do we always come to visit Pepi? I ask my father. Why can't she come and visit us?

We live in a nice house, Mishkenot Sha'ananim, a private guesthouse for artists. We have our own garden, which faces Jaffa Gate and the Dome of the Rock.

Pepi can come over whenever she wants to, my father answers. But she won't.

Why not?

Because she's old. And tired. Anyway, why would she want to come over? It's easier for me to come and visit her.

I think you should invite her over with some of your friends. She might enjoy it.

Don't tell me what to do. You're a child. You don't know anything about the world.

I'm not a child, I'm twelve years old.

My father laughs sardonically. Twelve years old is a child, he says.

Maybe, I mutter. Well, child or not, I just thought Pepi might enjoy coming over to our house for a change.

She won't.

Why?

My father pauses.

Because I say so.

According to my father, only the highest achievers can mix with each other. *Ils doivent avoir quelque chose en commun.* They must have something in common.

As for the possibility that a disparate mix of achievers and lesser mortals might find something in common during conversation?

No. No such thing.

Those who only have my parents' friendship in common are relegated to an occasional tea, or a dinner-party invitation. On

their own.
No mixes there.
Dinner – always impressive, always accompanied by a good bottle of wine – will be prepared diligently by my mother.
Soup – hot or cold – followed by chicken, or fish, served with a sophisticated gratin of vegetables and wild rice. A large cheese platter will be served. Always. Dessert – fruit sorbet or home-made cake – will usually be followed by a cup of herbal tea, *une petite tisane*, in the living room.
By that time Noga and I are asleep, although occasionally I am awoken by the sound of laughter, or the clang of dishes coming from the kitchen.

Pepi has never been to Paris.
I imagine her walking into a café near the Luxembourg Gardens. She sits down, careful not to crease her skirt, and orders a cup of tea.
The waiter arrives and places the cup and saucer in front of her, together with some milk and sugar.
I didn't ask for milk, she protests, meekly.
But the waiter doesn't hear her.
So she removes the sugar from its wrapper, slips the two lumps into her hot tea, and sips it gently. Very gently.
As she watches a few mothers returning from the Luxembourg, holding their children by the hand, her eyes well up with tears again.
She was once like them.
She wore lipstick and French perfume. She held her children by the hand and cooked them special recipes at home.
She had nice clothes and little ambition, but it didn't matter.

Life wasn't about ambition, but contentment. And she had plenty of that.

Pepi removes a compact from her handbag and checks her face in the mirror. She applies some powder to her cheeks and chin, a touch of lipstick to her lips.
There. Much better.
Then, she stands up, pays for her tea and walks slowly back to our apartment.

Alba! I'm talking to you!
My father interrupts my thoughts.
We have to leave. Say goodbye to Pepi.

We kiss and she hugs me again. No tears, this time.
We've barely spoken to each other. But then again, we hardly ever do.
The timeless, tacit complicity of blood ties.

A taxi driver picks us up. He's smoking a cigarette and Israeli music is blaring from the front seat.
Please, no cigarettes, no music, my father says.
The driver throws his cigarette out of the window and turns the music off, grudgingly.
We drive off into the Jerusalem sunset.

2

The bus ride from west Jerusalem to Tel Arza takes an hour. Noga and I are on our way to visit our maternal grandmother, Savta. She lives in an Orthodox community, near the Biblical Zoo.

Against my mother's wishes, I am dressed in a T-shirt and shorts. At least I can wear shorts with my back brace, although the double T-shirt and scarf somewhat diminish the intended impact: bare arms, bare legs.

You want to provoke these people? my father asks me, before I leave the house. It is Noga's and my first bus trip alone.

No, I don't want to provoke them, I lie. It's hot here, and I'm not going to wear a long dress.

You suffer the consequences. I don't care, he says.

My father has an aversion to Orthodox Jews. To my grandmother whom he always derides.

Ignorant woman, he says. Unaesthetic woman.

Stop it. Not in front of the girls, my mother says.

I don't understand how you could have been the product of such a family, my father tells her.

My father was an elegant man, my mother states firmly.

Maybe, my father retorts. But your mother isn't an elegant woman.

As the bus gets closer to its Orthodox destination, out go the young students, the soldiers in their khaki uniforms, the fashionable women, the amorous couples, and in come those in Orthodox garb. A plethora of wigs and kerchiefs, of broad-brimmed hats and forelocks, of loud children and tired mothers. Many have drawn faces and ungainly long dresses which reveal the tip of a cheap shoe. Or a ripped stocking.

Occasionally, elegant women enter the bus midway through the trip. Their shapely dresses and high necklines are complemented by dainty make-up, an expensive ring sitting atop a creamy finger. I stare at them without compunction and they stare back. Where do you live? I feel like asking them. And why did you choose to live this way?

I am witnessing a moment in a life of religious compromise and sartorial restriction, so far from my Parisian roots that the difference is exotic. Yet, where I should feel some form of empathy, or respect, I feel an impulsive desire to taunt them.

Let's pull that woman's kerchief off her head right before we get off the bus, I tell my sister, pointing towards the middle-aged woman who is sitting in front of us, loudly reprimanding a small boy in Yiddish. His sleeping sibling sucks his thumb in a pushchair. At one point, he wakes up and the mother lifts him up, revealing wet armpits. I can smell her sweat from my seat.

Come on, let's do it, I repeat.
Are you crazy? my sister asks.
I dare you. I promise you a present if you do it with me.
I often bribe my sister but don't always keep my promises.
No. I don't want to. We'll get into trouble. And why would you want to do it? It's mean.

It's not mean, it's fun.
No, it's not.
Never mind, you chicken. I'll do it alone.
As the bus reaches its final stop, I reach out towards the woman's kerchief.
Don't do it, everyone is looking at you, my sister whispers.
I don't care, I answer, as my hand begins to tremble.

The woman gets up as my hand is touching the fabric on her head. It feels soft.
Too late, I tell my sister. She got up before I could do it, that stupid woman.
Next time. You'll do it next time.

A few boys in dirty clothing and long forelocks throw stones at me as we get off the bus. An older man reprimands me. Where do you think you are, dressed like this? he asks me. My sister is worried. You're going to get us killed, she whispers.
Don't be stupid, I answer haughtily. But secretly, I wonder.

Savta is kind enough to ignore my bare legs. She presses us against her bosom and kisses us too many times. Oy, that metal instrument you have to carry on your back, she tells me. Why do you need to wear such a thing? Oy, never mind she adds, before I can even answer her. You are beautiful girls, the two of you. Beautiful girls. Beautiful *meydales* she repeats, in her Yiddish accent.

She wears a kerchief on her head, a long tunic and slippers. Her apartment smells of food. Pickles and stuffed peppers,

schnitzel and coleslaw, and something unpleasant. Her medicine cabinet? I know it holds expired tablets and dubious-looking potions which she refuses to discard. I need them for my old body, she says. My tired muscles.
So she does. And so the afternoon will roll by. She will ask us the same questions, over and over again.
How is your health?
How is school?
How is your mother?
How is your Hebrew?
How is your father?
Have some more food.

More. You're too thin. You should eat more. Here, have some more food. What does she feed you that daughter of mine? You don't want any more? (we shake our heads). OK, so don't have any more, *vat* can I do . . .

After lunch, she shows us pictures of the family. My grandfather, Joseph, who died many years before. A tall, handsome man with a long beard and a gentle face. My mother looks like him. They have the same dark hair and green, oriental eyes.
Joseph, a very devout man, awoke every morning at five o'clock to read the Bible before taking the subway from Brooklyn to Manhattan, where he was a kosher meat supervisor. He was a learned man, and sang beautifully, my mother told me. Our house was always full of song. We may have been poor, but we had music.

Kosher meat supervisor and spiritual figure.

I envision Joseph with his apron tied around his waist, taking notes as the butcher rinses the meat three times before stamping the kosher certificate on its skin.

Seven circles around a bride.
Seven circles around a corpse.
Three shovels of earth on a closed coffin.
Raw flesh and blood watered down three times.

Baruch ata Adonai, Joseph recites, his body swaying back and forth, his eyes glued to the small, black Bible print.
Joseph speaks Hebrew like a native. Eight generations of forefathers have guaranteed that the language of his ancestors will never desert him.
Savta is different. Her ancestry is foggy and she has had little education. Hebrew may be in her blood, but not in her diction. As a result, when she speaks, she sounds as if she comes from nowhere in particular.

There are pictures of my mother, as a child. Of her three brothers, standing on a street somewhere in Williamsburg, Brooklyn, *circa* 1949. There is, however, no photograph of their sister, who died when she was a child. The cause of death was never determined.
Savta doesn't mention her and we never ask.

3

Joseph and Savta moved to Jerusalem from New York in the 1960s, after Joseph had retired from his job as a meat supervisor. We visited once, with my recalcitrant father. Noga was a baby, I was four years old.

A tall man with a beard picked me up affectionately. Savta served home-made pastries.

It was the only time my father visited their home.

What a terrible place, he said.

Joseph died a few months later, of Parkinson's disease. He was sixty-eight years old.

My grandfather was a good-looking man. I imagine that on his wedding day, when he lifted his wife's veil and discovered her plain features, he must have felt a pang of disappointment.

Then again, being a devout Jew, Joseph had presumably accepted his fate as God's will; if this was the woman he was to marry, he would make the best of it.

Joseph and Savta settled in Jerusalem. Their first son was born in the early 1920s. At the age of two, he died in the typhus epidemic which was ravaging the city.

Another son was born in 1924, a daughter two years later.

Joseph found a job in a Jewish publication company, which printed poems, books and pamphlets.

One day, his eyes fell upon a poem which disputed God's existence.

How could he print such blasphemous material?
He discarded the poem and moved on to the next book.

A few weeks later, the same thing happened.
When confronted by his superior, Joseph declared that he could not possibly print any kind of literature which denied the existence of God.
In that case, you must leave, his superior said.
Joseph tried to argue his case, but in vain.

He went to New York for four years, occasionally returning to Jerusalem. He found a few odd jobs here and there, including working for the Irgun, a militant Zionist group, helping ship arms to Israel.
Every return to Jerusalem produced another child. And every child meant another expense.

During the same period, Schlomo turned to his brother Joseph for help.
Schlomo studied the Kabbalah all day and didn't work.
Help me feed my seven children, he said.

Joseph obliged. He felt a duty towards his brother.
Study is the highest form of prayer.
But prayers don't pay the bills.

Five children later, Joseph decided to leave Israel for good.
Come and join me in a few months, he told his family.
Savta was reluctant to leave. But she had to obey her husband.
In 1938, right before the advent of penicillin, and a few weeks

before the family was about to embark on the SS *Normandie* for America, my mother's sister died; she was twelve years old.

The family left Palestine with her name and picture on their group passport.
Joseph only found out about his elder daughter's death when the family arrived in New York.
He never forgave himself for it.

I was told her name, once. Then I was asked to forget it.
But I didn't.

4

Tessa and I enter the Old City through the Jaffa Gate. We follow a maze of small streets, all the way to the Arab quarter.
I know Tessa from many years back. Our mothers went to high school together, in Brooklyn. Tessa, three years older than me, lives in Manhattan, but her father lives in Israel and she visits him every summer.
Until recently, Tessa didn't acknowledge my presence, except for when her mother was around. These days, she'll only see me when her mother's not around.
You're a mature twelve-year-old, she says.
I'm delighted.
In a café by the souk entrance, two men wearing *kafiahs* on their heads drink mint tea while loud Arab music can be heard in the background. A boy sells sesame bread from a cart. Tessa

and I buy a piece and share it on the steps. The dough feels warm and crispy.
A woman comes out of the café wearing a blue embroidered kaftan, gold bangles on her wrists. A dark braid dangles below her waistline.
She's beautiful, I remark.
Tessa shrugs her shoulders. You think so?
Tessa has long black hair, olive skin and long legs. When she laughs, she crinkles her nose. She speaks quickly and looks older than her fifteen years. I notice that men look at her as we walk by.
I envy her. I hate my thick, frizzy hair, my pimply face, my wiry legs
As we venture inside the souk, a man stops us, trying to sell his wares. My friends! he cries out, pointing towards a ceramic shop. Beautiful things for you! Good prices!
Follow me, Tessa says. I'm going to take you to a jewellery shop owned by a Moroccan woman I know. Leila. She lives alone with her two children.
Tessa then tells me about her eighteen-year-old boyfriend who is training to be an army pilot.
My father hates him, she says. He says he's too old for me.
She shrugs her shoulders again. But it doesn't matter, because I never listen to my parents.
I shrug my shoulders back. Neither do I.

We walk past an old Arab woman, sitting on the ground, surrounded by watermelons. Her legs are spread out in front of her and her toenails are black. She smiles at us as we pass by. Red gums, no teeth.

Surrounded by the smell of cardamom, sage and fresh fish from the nearby stalls, she empties a watermelon of its pulp and methodically throws the seeds into a small bag by her side. There is something engrossing about watching her coarse hands as they move swiftly between the bag and the pulp.
Let's go, says Tessa tugging at my sleeve. The shop will close soon.

We never find the shop, or its Moroccan owner. Instead, we get lost in the maze of the Old City, our hearts beating fast as the sun starts to set and the call of the muezzin resonates within the city walls.

5

Israel is where we spend every summer but Paris is our home. We live in a flat on the border of the 13th arrondissement, between the Boulevard Montparnasse and the Luxembourg Gardens. We attend the École Alsacienne, a fashionable private school. I struggle there and so does my sister. My grades are poor and my lack of friends stirs me to invent a few whom I actually pretend to go and visit, circling our apartment block over and over again, until a reassuring couple of hours later I can safely return home, where I enthusiastically recount my visit to N's house, on the Boulevard Arago. Occasionally I will embellish my accounts with tales about N's hippie parents, which invariably leads my father to vent his tirades about 1968 and the irretrievable demise of French values.

My refuge is my imagination. The world of words and images to which my parents belong. There is, according to my father, no other acceptable world to belong to. Purity, in its most refined form, is what we must all aspire to. And this aspiration pays our bills; whereas my mother's poetry has become an infrequent occupation, my father's studio is set up a few feet away from our front entrance. It is from there that he produces most of his work.

Our flat has been immortalised on canvas.
The bedrooms, the kitchen, the balcony, the living room.
Ourselves. As infants, toddlers, teenagers. My mother from the front and the back, sitting and standing, reclining and sleeping.
My father. Self-portraits in the nude, dressed, shouting, pensive, tired.
The views from outside. The neighbour's flat at number 10. The views on to the garden of the Augustine nuns. The square itself.
The objects. Sculptures, fruit, flowers, books, towels, ceilings and cracked walls.
The people. Sam, especially. Head lowered, smoking a cigar, gazing into the horizon, talking and smiling.
Others, too. Writers and painters, musicians and actors, politicians and historians.
Everyday people. Passengers on trains and subways, down-trodden characters, street musicians and lovers, or simply passers-by sketched with a quick pencil line.

Sometimes, a month or two can go by without him painting

anything. These are usually the worst times when we become victims of his increasing frustration.
Then suddenly, when the tension has become so palpable as to become unendurable, inspiration will come to the rescue.
My father turns on the music. Beethoven's *Eroica* or Glenn Gould playing the *Goldberg Variations*.
He closes the studio door and disappears for a few hours, while a reverent silence descends upon us all.

Hush. Walk on tiptoe. Respect your father. No sound. Little movement.

When he emerges from his studio brandishing his brush and looking utterly dishevelled, Noga and I are asked to assess the finished product. Is it good?
We nod, enthusiastically.
No, it's not good, he says. It's shit.
No! we exclaim.
Oh, I don't know.
But it's good! We exclaim, again.
OK, maybe. Or maybe not . . .
It's wonderful, darling, my mother says, in her soothing voice, as she walks into the room. Absolutely wonderful.
Is it? Maybe it is. Maybe it's good. If you say so.
All I want to do then is run. Back to my room, my diary, my pre-pubescent world. Adults are not supposed to harbour doubts, nor demonstrate vulnerability. Adults are supposed to know all the answers. Adults are sturdy and reliable, like brick walls. They might not be able to prevent every fall, but will always help us back up if we do.

My father doesn't forgive falls. You must be strong and resilient, he says. You must think before you act.
You cannot fall.

In October 1941, your father's childhood was taken away from him, my mother once told me.
Taken away by men in pale grey uniform who stacked him and his family into a cattle wagon and drove them to a place of no return.

I heard those words before, spoken by a woman on television, part of a documentary on Holocaust survivors.
In 1942, the Germans took my mother away from me, the woman said. I was holding her hand, and then I wasn't. They ripped us apart, like clothing. I was six years old.
I ran after her and she slapped me hard on the cheek. Get away, she said. Don't come after me.
I never saw my mother again. She had gone to a place of no return.
And I hadn't.

When I was ten years old, my father called me into his studio and showed me a large stack of drawings.
You see these? he said. Well, I need to do a selection here and I'd like you to help me. I'd like you to give me your opinion on the drawings I should save, and the ones I should burn.
Burn?
Yes, burn.
He lit a fire and spread the drawings out around us. Nearly

one hundred of them, in all shapes and sizes. I felt a mixture of pride and fear. My father had asked me for my opinion. But what if I was wrong? What if I burned the wrong ones? What would happen then?
I trust your eye. You know that.

We began the process of elimination. The fire smouldered and crackled while I was asked to give a yes or a no.
Yes.
Drawing stacked carefully into a corner.
No.
Throwing sheets of Chinese paper into the fire, watching them turn to dust.
We talked. We joked. We laughed.
We began throwing them faster and faster, until by the time we were done, seventy drawings were up in smoke. Thousands of dollars of living expenses up in smoke.

6

Noga and I sleep in the same room.
Early one morning, I wake up to find her making strange noises. I look down from my double-decker bed. Her fists are clenched and bubbles are coming out of her mouth. I can't tell whether her eyes are open, or closed.
Noga? I call out.
She doesn't answer.
I jump out of bed, race out of the room and into my parents' bedroom.

Something's not right with Noga, I say.
My father rushes in and takes her temperature. 41.9°.
One degree more and she could die, he says, haltingly.

My heart beats wildly.

The doctor is called. Shortly afterwards, an ambulance arrives and she is taken to hospital.
Noga has pneumonia, I am told. It's serious.
When she comes home a few days later, she seems smaller and frailer.
I hug her tightly. It's hard to let her go.

7

Our class is going on a trip. We travel to Lozère, by train. I share a dormitory with other girls. Annabelle, Barbara, Brigitte, Isabelle. Whereas in Paris they barely acknowledge my presence, here, in unknown territory, they do. My brace, a cause of derision at school, is seen here as an impediment worthy of some sort of pity. Annabelle decides to become my friend. So does Barbara, a Greek girl. Barbara is beautiful and popular with boys. One day, as we are eating lunch in the large cafeteria, she asks me which church I attend in Paris. I'm Jewish, I tell her. I don't go to church.
The Jews killed Jesus Christ. I cannot be your friend, she announces.

We milk cows in Lozère and visit the Cantal factory, where

they make cheese. We taste the cheese with our fingers and learn about the pasteurisation process. We walk for miles on country roads and learn how to light bonfires.

I don't take a shower for two weeks, and when I finally return to Paris, ecstatic about the trip, my parents tell me that I smell. So do all the other children and nothing could make me happier. We all smell because we chose to rebel against the communal showers. I was part of the rebellion. I became one of them.

United in stink.

III

Samuel Beckett is coming to dinner.
He is tall and gaunt, with sharp cheekbones and blue eyes like the sea.
As I have turned thirteen a few days before, he wishes me a happy birthday and kisses me on both cheeks. No present, however. So much for his godfatherly duties. Then again, he is no ordinary godfather and he never shirked on presents before. On the contrary. His generosity towards me has always been laudable.
Do you realise what this means? My father often reminds me. Do you understand the significance of Sam's gifts?
Yes, I do.
No, you don't. I'm holding on to them until you're able to understand their value.
You don't need to. I understand their value.
No, you don't. You're a child.

I'm not a child. I'm a young woman. I understand the significance of his gifts: a first edition of one of his novels. The silver spoon he had as a baby. A coral necklace which I've never worn.
But I don't understand the overbearing habit of highlighting a uniqueness I have recognised on my own.

Sam follows my father into the living room. He pulls out a

sheet of paper and hands it over to me. Happy birthday, he says.
So he did remember, after all. I shouldn't have doubted him.
I hold the typescript in my hand. *Il fut trouvé par terre.* It was found on the ground. I look at Sam and smile. Thank you, I say.
He smiles back. It's just one page.
A special page.

A bottle of Jameson whiskey is opened. My father and Sam talk about his latest play, while my mother prepares dinner in the kitchen. Noga follows us into the living room.
My father puts on a Schubert sonata and tells me to be quiet.
Noga sits still while I fidget in my chair. I can hear pots and pans being rattled around in the kitchen.
Don't talk while the music is on, I am warned.
He then proceeds to close his eyes while Sam remains motionless.
I squirm in my seat until my father orders me to leave the room.
I ask Noga if she'll follow me. I want to stay here, she says.
Fine.

I rush off to the bathroom and apply grey eyeshadow to my eyelids, then wipe it off. No make-up allowed at home. Not at thirteen years old. Too young, still.
How come Noga is so different from me? I wonder.
No rock music for her. Or make-up. Or fits of anger.
If Noga bears any grudges towards us, she keeps them to herself. She is quiet, often pensive. She has declared that when she's older, she will be an astronomer.

She receives a telescope for her birthday and she plants it on our balcony, in the hope of spotting a few stars.
What we do spot is the intimate lives of our neighbours. We see them undressing, talking and laughing. We forget all about the stars; this is better than anything we could have imagined. We giggle and focus the lens on those neighbours we like the least, until my mother catches us in the act and puts an abrupt end to our clandestine activity.

Before Noga goes to sleep, she clears her desk and sets her pens and pencils next to each other, with firm instructions to us all not to move them without her consent.
She places her shoes by the bed with painstaking precision, her laces stretched out in perfect parallels.
She slips under the sheets, barely touching them and often, by morning, it is hard to determine whether someone actually slept there the night before.
This fills my father with joy and me with horror.
You're such a freak maniac, I tell her.
She shrugs her shoulders. I don't care if I am.

When Noga has conversations with my father, her questions are neatly formulated, her answers pondered upon at great length. They discuss thoughts and deeds performed centuries ago. They have few dealings with the present, but much to uncover about the mysteries of the past.
My father listens to Noga and she to him. They sit and talk quietly. She neither fights nor judges him. He'll never change, she once said to me, so what's the point?

Somehow, I know she's right. But in order to affirm my identity, I still need to fight him back. We rarely sit and talk quietly. Most of the time, we stand up and argue.
Why don't you ever listen to me? he shouts. I'm telling you about David, one of the greatest painters who ever lived!
I'm listening! I shout back.

But I'm not. I'm more interested in how people lived, as opposed to what they accomplished. I'm interested in what they couldn't say and those feelings they didn't share.
It must have been harder then, to share feelings.

Although we live in the same house and share the same parents, Noga and I don't share our intimate thoughts. I keep my school life to myself, and so does she. She knows a few of my friends, having met them at home, but seems oblivious to their presence, perhaps in anticipation of my mocking her in public, or simply because she doesn't really care.

I, however, am curious about Noga's friends. There is Ariane, with curly blonde hair and a childish voice. Elise, an only child, whose mother is a baker. Sometimes I eavesdrop behind Noga's bedroom door, in the hope of catching a snippet of their conversation. Perhaps the public Noga will reveal something to me which I don't know in private.
Is she angry, like me? Is she sad? Is she happy?
I never get to know. Their conversations are surprisingly mundane and so are their activities. Playing with Noga's chemistry set. Elise commenting on some famous French rock singer. Noga discussing her love of animals.

So after a while, I give up on eavesdropping altogether.

Sam follows me into my bedroom and sits at the piano with me. I play him a Mozart sonata. I know that piece, he says. His voice is low and raspy.
He tries playing too, although his right hand is hampered by a muscular disease.

We sit down for dinner. Your eyes look puffy, my mother remarks.
Fish is served and Sam swallows the fish bones. Calcium, he says.
He recounts a trip to Dublin. A few people he saw, places he revisited. My father asks him about the new production of his play, *Happy Days*. Their friend in London, Jocelyn, designed the set.
My mother wheels in a plate of cheeses. Sam recites a Shakespeare sonnet, then Keats. *Ode to a Nightingale.* My mother joins in, while my father grins throughout.
I must go and finish my homework, I announce, after dessert is served.
We discuss homework and school. Sam asks a few questions, I answer evasively. I cannot wait for dinner to end.

A man like Sam comes along every three hundred years, my father tells me, later on.
Do you understand what it means to have such a man in your life?
Is it about meaning? I ask.
Of course it is, he retorts.

2

Every morning, my father tunes into the Israeli news on his radio, a small brown leather transistor with a red dial.
Kol Israel, short wave, long distance.
A man's voice booms around the room, often echoed by my father's loud interjections.
The news is interspersed with advertisements and songs, usually Israeli folk music which, if she happens to hear it, will bring immediate tears to my mother's eyes.
If there happens to be an upheaval in the country, my father and mother will sit around the kitchen table with a look of utmost concentration, followed by several phone calls to their friend Naomi, in Jerusalem.
Is everyone OK? Was anyone hurt?
My father rants and raves. About Menachem Begin. The horrible Likud. *Ayom ve nora.* Terrible and horrible. Shameful to have a man like that in power.
Shameful.

Then, there is *France Culture* and *France Musique*, which are switched on daily.

Be quiet. We're listening. You should listen too. This is very interesting. Very beautiful.

I don't. I listen when I want to, not when I'm told to.
Then again, I'm always told to.
It's not about what I want.

Often in France, when there is a political or cultural matter to be resolved, the writers and philosophers are called in.
They are taken very seriously and some of them are as famous as movie stars.
They declaim their opinions in bombastic voices and sound very self-assured.
There is something very appealing about the idea of a thinker or a writer being as popular as an actor or a singer.
Them, I listen to.

Except that most of the time I don't understand a word they say.

3

My father gives me a stamp collection. I used to enjoy doing this as a young boy, he says.
For once, I can see why.
I lose myself in countries with exotic names and colourful illustrations. Magyar. Republic of Burundi. Upper Volta. Ceylon.
I place them carefully in my album. I study the countries and their people.
If I cannot travel to these destinations, at least I can dream of them.
Except for dictatorships.
From their stamps alone, I would never know. Their illustrations are rarely indicative of a repressive regime.

4

There is a concert at school. I am asked to participate.

I choose a piece with my piano teacher, an ebullient Israeli woman. We decide on a Chopin prelude. I practise day and night. This is my first recital, and I am terrified. What if I am taunted? Or laughed at?

The night of the recital I tell my mother that I feel ill. But she convinces me to go.

I am one of the first. I always am. First letter, all around. I am doubly cursed with my name.

Alba Arikha will be playing Chopin, a woman announces.

A few sneers.

I sit at the piano, my brace against my back, my glasses slipping down my sweaty nose.

Somehow or another, I manage to play. The notes become colours, as they often do when I lose myself in music. A is yellow, B-flat dark blue. C is white. G is black. As for F-sharp, a light green. Colours flying around the keyboard, a rainbow of undulating sounds.

A silence descends upon the audience. Why are they so quiet?

Then, the applause. Unexpected and loud.

I get up and return to my seat, past a stream of coughs and claps. A few children look at me. You play really well, they say.

My first public victory.

5

A sweltering day in Jerusalem. Tessa and I walk past the cheap hardware and clothing stores on Jaffa Street, the falafel stands, the cafés with their radios on full blast. A bus pulls up at its stop and a corpulent man attempts to shove his way to the front of the queue, only to be met by an irate crowd of passengers. A fight erupts and the street comes to a momentary standstill before the bus finally pulls away.

Tessa grabs my hand. I hate this street, she says. We'll get there another way. Follow me.

We turn left on a side street with beautiful stone houses, carved wooden doors and wrought-iron window grilles. On one balcony, a woman with curlers in her hair is hanging laundry on a clothes-line.

You see that house? Tessa says, pointing towards the woman.

Yes.

It used to belong to Arabs. Hundreds of them were thrown out in 1948 and the Israelis moved in. That woman should not be living there. It's wrong.

I nod. My father has told me about this before. We were offered a house which he refused to live in, because it had once belonged to an Arab family.

Did the Arabs ever try to return? I ask. To claim their house back, I mean.

Tessa looks at me snidely. How do you want them to come back? Do you think the Israelis will say, sure, why don't you move back in, we'll get the keys copied for you?

I suppose not, I answer, feeling my cheeks redden.

She looks at me harshly. I suppose not either.

She pauses and looks at me again. Do you know a little about Israeli politics?

A little, I mumble. Not much.
When I'm older, I want to go into politics. Tessa's tone has gained momentum and she now speaks feverishly.
I want to change the way things are between people. I want to see peace. What happened to the Arabs was wrong. I want to make the world a better and fairer place. This is my goal.

I hope you achieve it, I say, feeling a mixture of reverence and despondency in the face of such determination. I hold no firm opinions. I know nothing about politics. I never thought about how I could bring about peace or change the world. How could I? I barely understand the world as it is.

We enter a jewellery shop. Tessa introduces me.
Dorit, this is my friend Alba. She's from Paris.
Dorit nods her head wearily. Paris. OK.
She wears a kerchief on her head and rouge on her cheeks.
You sit here, she says, tapping on a small stool. And don't move.
With an instrument resembling a small pistol she pierces my ears and tells me to disinfect them every evening.
We pay her and leave quickly; Tessa has an appointment with her boyfriend, Ronnen. Do you want to meet him? she asks.
Sure, I answer.
We walk to Ben Yehuda Street. It is filled with American backpacking tourists and students. A man with long hair and a white bandanna, a guitar strapped around his shoulders, sings a Neil Young song with his eyes closed.
We sit on white plastic chairs in a sidewalk café. Everyone around us is smoking. Israeli rock 'n' roll is blasting from the

back room. Tessa sings along. I love this song, she says. We order Coca-Cola while she sways her body to the music.

I stare at her. I wouldn't know how to sway my body even if I was asked to. I've got a long way to go, I decide, as a good-looking Israeli soldier stops in front of us. He is dressed in the standard olive-green army uniform, black leather boots, a rifle held at his waist.

Hey, he says.

Hey, Tessa says back, blushing slightly.

She introduces us. Ronnen, Alba.

He sits down and puts his arm around Tessa.

They start talking to each other, ignoring me. Tessa's Hebrew is fluent, unlike mine.

Ronnen wants to be a pilot she tells me, as he pulls out a cigarette.

So you said, I feel like saying. Their presence is jarring. As if I were watching something prohibited.

Ronnen takes a puff of his cigarette, and twirls a strand of Tessa's long hair between his fingers. She beams at him. He kisses her cheek, then the back of her neck.

Has he seen her naked? I wonder.

I have to go, I say, feeling increasingly queasy.

No, wait! Tessa protests meekly.

Really.

I get up and leave. There is no point in my staying with them. They clearly want to be alone.

And so do I.

Little golden studs adorn my thirteen-year-old ears. The scarf around my back brace is soaked with perspiration and I remove

it on the street, revealing the pink, plastic contraption around my neck.
A few people stare at me but I don't mind. I have pierced ears now so it no longer matters.

I spend the afternoon in the local day camp at the YMCA. I fumble with my Hebrew and am delighted to make a new friend, Sarah.

She tells me that her parents are divorced. Her mother is English and her Israeli father, whom she never sees, lives in New York.
I tell Sarah about my family. When I mention my father's name she becomes agitated. But he's famous! she says.
So he is.

By the end of the afternoon we know all there is to know about each other. Our favourite rock bands. Our school crushes. Our parents. Our siblings. The girls we hate in the day camp and those we look up to. I tell her about Tessa and how precocious she seems. I'm sure they did it, I say.
In Israel, people do it early, Sarah declares. Right after high school we have to join the army, and we never know what's going to happen next. The whole country could blow up, who knows. So we do it early and we marry early. And then, we divorce early too, she adds, with a note of sarcasm in her voice.
I see, I answer, slightly overwhelmed by the notion of the whole country blowing up.
Well, tomorrow I'm seeing Ilan, I tell her, speaking quickly.

He's fifteen years old, the son of my father's friend, Ofer. I think I'm in love with him.
Sarah nods her head gravely. I think I'm in love with my boyfriend too. You'll meet him when you come to my house. Come and stay over next weekend. I'll ask my mother, you ask yours.

6

We are in the car with Naomi and Charles, driving to Ma'ale Ha-hamisha, a kibbutz west of Jerusalem. My father lived there for five years, when he first arrived in Palestine, in 1944. The sun is hotter than usual, and I can feel it burning my shoulders through the open window. Once we leave Jerusalem, the landscape quickly becomes mountainous, a sprawl of white rock, pine trees and dust.
Noga and I begin to quarrel and my father tells us to be quiet. Charles keeps his eyes on the road and doesn't say much.
He is very tall, so much so that Noga and I need to stand on tiptoe to distinguish his features. Angular face, small eyes hidden behind large frames, a mane of white hair.
Charles and Naomi live in a beautiful house with a pool and a large garden. They throw expansive lunches that last all afternoon, and which include children as well as older people. Everything in their house seems easy and carefree.
My father knew Naomi when they were both young and somehow this connection, the past they shared before my time, renders the relationship more special. I cannot judge them because, just like family members, they have always been in

our lives. To me, any connection to the past is valuable.

But not to my father.

As we approach our destination, he becomes nervous.

Why are we here? Why do I have to see these people again? I have nothing to say to them, do you hear? Nothing.

You wanted to show the kibbutz to the girls, didn't you? My mother says, in her comforting voice.

Yes, maybe, he grumbles.

Anyway, this looks familiar, I say.

I recognise the white, modern building in front of me. We came to visit, a few years back.

We sat in the cafeteria, which smelled of bad food. A kind lady gave me freshly prepared carrot juice. A few people came to speak to me as if they knew me. In Israel, unlike in France, being my father's daughter gives me added kudos. I am special because I am his daughter.

No other reason.

As the car winds its way along a dusty road, we pass an older man, who raises his hand in salutation.

Do you know him? Naomi asks my father.

Yes. We were in the camps together.

He had a nice face, my mother says.

But don't you want to say hello? To speak to him? I exclaim.

No. Why would I? All we had in common was the camps and this place. He's never read a book in his life. He knows nothing about art. I have nothing to say to him.

But you were in the camps together! I shout. Isn't that plenty?

Will you stop this! My father shouts back. There are some things you're too young to understand!

My mother turns around and looks at me with worried eyes.

Don't get your father upset, she says quickly. Not here.
Naomi acquiesces. It's your father's choice. You shouldn't insist.

I feel the anger boil inside me. Everything is about my father. His history sits between us like an intruder who will never leave.
I should be somewhere else. Not here.
The heat is suffocating me. The atmosphere is suffocating me.
One day, I will leave.
I will become the reverse of what I am.

7

The following day, we go to tea at Ilan's parents' house. I leave my brace behind.
I apply some kohl around my eyes and dab my pimples with a pink lotion, in a desperate and futile attempt at hiding them.
I wear a flowery dress and open-toed sandals, which I found in the Old City.
My father calls a taxi. My mother squeezes my hand. I can tell that you put eyeliner on, she whispers, but don't worry, I won't tell your father.

Thank you, I whisper back.

We arrive at Dafna and Ofer's house.
Dafna has cooked a pound cake. Ofer smokes a large cigar in the garden. He greets us effusively and hugs my sister and me.
Beautiful girls, he tells my mother.

I roll my eyes.

He puts his arm around my father's shoulder and they begin a conversation about his recent scientific discovery.
Dafna offers us some cake and pours hot water into a teapot.
She hands my mother a teacup.
Dafna is big. Big chest, big arms, big voice. Her face, though, is beautiful.
She was stunning when she was young, my father tells me.
And so was Ofer, my mother declares. They were a very good-looking couple.

There is something mysterious about the dynamics of ageing.
About catching a fleeting glimpse of the past in aged faces.
Flesh leaves clues.
Like on Savta.
A dimple amidst a wrinkle. A sparkling eye. A hearty laugh.
Savta aged gracefully. So did Pepi, despite her suffering.
Easier to detect pain in a word than a face.

Tea? Dafna asks us.
No tea. Juice please.
She walks towards the kitchen and comes back with a jug of juice, pouring two glasses for my sister and me.
How are you girls? she asks, in a loud voice.
Fine, we're fine.

Dafna wraps her skirt underneath her voluptuous bottom as she snuggles up next to my mother on a sofa. They bring their

heads together and Dafna mutters something indistinct.
Is she talking about me? About Noga? About Ilan?
I barely nibble on my cake, wondering where he is.
Where are the boys? My mother asks, holding the teacup gently in her hand. She sips her tea carefully, as if she were afraid of breaking the cup.

Does she know?
No. She couldn't.

I pour myself more orange juice as I wait for Dafna's answer.
Can I have some more too? Noga asks.
I sigh loudly and complain about her not being able to do things on her own.
Ezer is in the army, Dafna says from across the room. Ilan will be back soon, he wanted to see you.

You.
Who? Me? Them?

I see a figure outside, through the living-room window.
Ilan.
He fumbles for his keys, then opens the front door and slams it a little too loudly.
I can feel my heartbeat rip through the fabric of my dress.
Ilan steps into the room and smiles widely at us. He kisses my mother, then his. He turns towards us, taller than I remembered, wearing a white T-shirt, army boots and torn jeans. His dark hair covers some of his face.

His beauty hurts.
He focuses his brown eyes on me and smiles a white-toothed smile. My glass of juice tilts precariously towards the floor.
How are you, Alba? he asks gently.
Oh, fine.

He sits down next to me and we engage in a conversation. Paris, Jerusalem, school. Do you still play the piano? he asks.
I nod.
You should play for me sometime, he murmurs.
His words melt on his tongue, like sugar.

Sure, I mumble indistinctly.

My brother plays the saxophone, he's really good, Ilan continues. He's been asked to join the National Youth Band.

National Youth Band.
The words sound like a tin drum.
Although Noga seems to disagree.
Wow! she exclaims from the other side of the room. He plays in a youth band!
I stare at her coldly. Shut up, I mouth, when Ilan gets up to pour himself a glass of juice.
I focus on his face, his uncanny resemblance to Gary Cooper. I have pictures of Gary Cooper pinned across the wall of my Paris bedroom. Gregory Peck too. And Alain Delon.

Ilan will never love me.
He's three years older than me. A friend of my parents once said that he had girlfriends lining up at his door.

I picture them. Young women lined up like clothes on a line, waiting to be kissed by him.

He will never kiss me.
For him, I simply do not exist. I am a pimply, gawky thirteen-year-old with frizzy hair and pale skin.
A lost cause.

If only he knew.

At school, I am taunted and teased for my brace and gawky looks, but also for the fact that I never fight back. I let insults hit me randomly, like pebbles. The thought of defending myself petrifies me. Why this is, I cannot say.
My body remains transfixed, as if I were undergoing an X-ray. Don't move! Don't breathe! an invisible technician orders me from inside his sealed booth.

Will it be different now that I'm older?

My assailants are mainly girls. A cluster of girls who crowd around me with large grins on their faces. I gather myself quickly once they walk away.
I know how to gather myself. Emotions are something I'm good at stashing away.
I have secrets.
Top-drawer secrets.
It's fine to expose my anger at home.
But not my pain.

That night, I dream of an empty landscape covered in soft dunes and golden sand. Miles and miles of sand, devoid of human life. The stillness is deafening.

A loud, male voice wakes me up. Alba.

Again. Alba.

I wake up with a start. There is no one there.

I lie in bed covered in sweat. Who could it be? Too loud to be a dream, too uncanny to be real.

Am I losing my mind? Hearing voices?

I toss and turn all night, but never find the answer.

8

We drive to Jericho at dawn with our friend Yaron and his girlfriend. Yaron is a curator at the Israel museum whom Noga and I have known since birth. An inveterate womaniser, he dresses in dapper clothes, smokes red Marlboros, speaks several languages and tells funny jokes. His girlfriend, Orna, is very shy. She has dark hair with a fringe and pale, slightly scaly skin. She seldom talks and when she does it's in a very quiet voice, as if she were afraid of being heard. My mother claims that she has many wise things to say and that it's a shame that she isn't more outspoken.

I tend to disagree. I don't think she has anything to say. Otherwise she would say it.

It's not that simple, my mother replies. Some people are insecure. Yaron overshadows her.

Why?

Because that's the way he is. He likes to be in control.

Sometimes at the expense of others, she adds.
Just like aba, I venture.
Aba's a good man, my mother states firmly.
And Yaron? Isn't he a good man?
She takes a while to answer. Yes, but he's naughtier, she finally declares.

Noga and I love naughty Yaron. One afternoon, when my parents are out, he offers to take us for a ride around Jerusalem. He swerves around on a dirt road, pretending we're on a ski slope.
We scream in mock terror and burst into fits of laughter.
We tell jokes and make fun of him.
He shows us places we've never seen before.
Hidden streets and monasteries.
An old Roman aqueduct.
On the way home, we stop for fruit popsicles and let the coloured syrup dribble down our chins.
We call Yaron our favourite uncle.

In the presence of my parents, Yaron is more contained.
He stops the car a few times to point out important sights. Herod's winter palace. St George's monastery. A cave where Byzantine monks once lived.

I roll down the window. The wind is hot. A smell of jasmine wafts in the air.
The road twists and turns as we climb up into the Judean mountains.

We arrive in Jericho around breakfast time.
We stop at a café. A middle-aged Arab man comes to greet us.
How are you my friend! he exclaims.
Yaron answers him in fluent Arabic.

He introduces us. Mustafa waves his arms enthusiastically and tells us to sit down.
He brings us orange juice, Turkish coffee for the adults, hummus and labneh for us all.
We dip warm pitta into the hummus while Arabic music plays in the background. An old man smokes a narghile outside.
The sun comes out, burning my bare shoulders. I close my eyes. I can feel the heat and dust stirring. The residue of last night's breeze.
A bee buzzes around me, insistently.
Yaron waves it away.
Go back to your mother, he tells the bee.
We laugh.

Mustafa looks at my sister and me. At my mother.
Pale girls, white skin, he tells her, pointing upwards.

Pale girls.

After breakfast, a young boy asks us if we'd like our shoes polished.
Yaron would.

The young man bends down and wipes them quickly with a cloth. He applies some polish and spits on them while Yaron smokes a cigarette.
I look on, fascinated.

When he's done, Yaron's shoes shine like mirrors.
Let's go, he says. He gives the young boy a crisp bill and stubs the cigarette out with his foot.
We pile back into his car, driving away into the dusty Jericho sun.

9

I spend a weekend at Sarah's house in the hills, outside Jerusalem. I tell my mother that I cannot bring my brace with me. Not this time, I say. I don't want to sleep over there with my back brace. She's my first Israeli friend, I add, feeding into her Zionist streak.
Fine, my mother relents.

I meet Sarah's boyfriend and a friend of his who takes me on the back of his motorcycle.
We run through the hills and jump over a few bushes. My body is free and limber.
We jump in a well, the main water supply to the local kibbutz. Keep your head low, I am told. If we're caught, we're dead.

I am thrilled.

Sarah and her boyfriend kiss on the side of the road. His friend looks at me.

I look away.

Sarah's mother cooks us *canard à l'orange* and her British stepfather, a magazine editor, asks me questions about my family. At night, we lie in bed and talk about our future. About our respective schools and about Sarah's boyfriend. I'm going to go on the pill when I turn fifteen, she announces gravely. But if my mother ever finds out she'll throw me out of the house.
The pill? At fifteen?
I'm not quite sure what to say. I don't have a boyfriend and I'm not about to go on the pill.
I kissed a boy, S, at a school dance. We kissed while slow dancing to an Eagles song, 'Hotel California'. Then, when the song was over, he walked me over to a chair and left me sitting there until it was time to go home.

After S, there was Bruno, a red-headed boy who lived on the Boulevard Raspail. He twirled his tongue inside my mouth and I wondered whether he was the one.
We sat on a park bench in the Luxembourg Gardens and kissed for hours, autumn leaves crackling beneath our feet.
Then we lit my first cigarette and I pretended to know what it was all about until the Luxembourg Gardens warden appeared with his whistle and ordered us to leave.
Out, or you'll be spending the night on the bench, he warned us.
We followed the warden and his peaked cap through the tall, black iron gates, as he blew his whistle continuously.
Bruno kissed me on the street.
I'll call you, he said.

IV

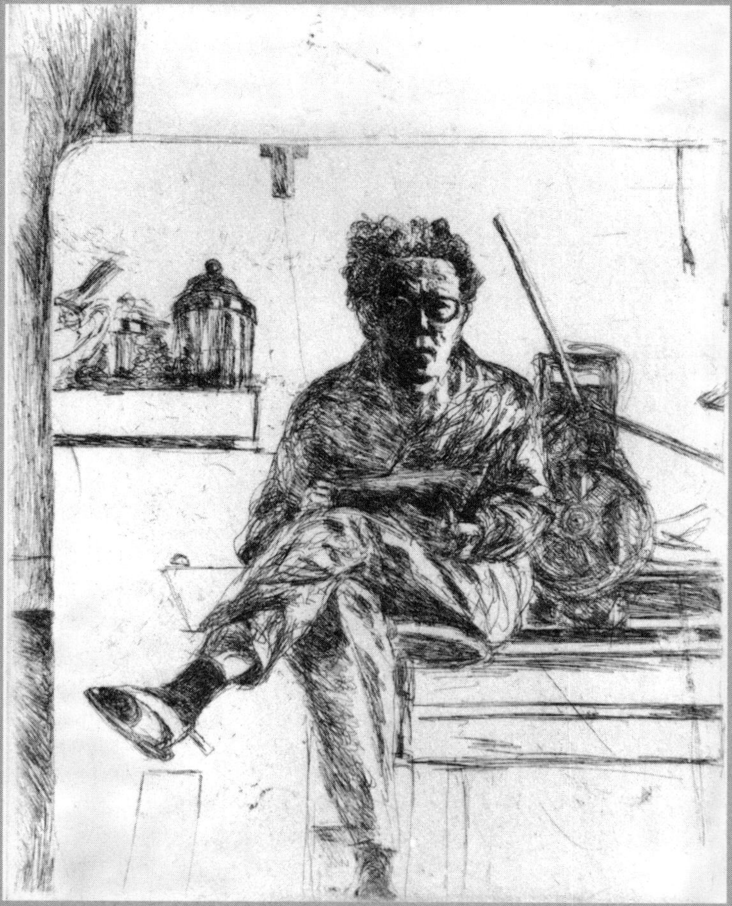

I am sitting in a café with my father, on the Boulevard de Port Royal. I am fifteen years old. For my birthday I received some new piano sheet music and was allowed to buy myself some new clothes.

It is a beautiful spring day and the terrace is filled with students and regulars, couples and older people who huddle in corners against the yellowing café walls.

My father is fidgety; he hates cafés.

Look at all those stupid smokers, he says, pointing around us. They don't realise what they're doing to themselves. They're killing themselves, these idiots. Killing themselves.

Yes, aba, I mutter.

A man reading the newspaper looks up at me and smiles. A pack of cigarettes lies in front of him. He sips his coffee from a white espresso cup.

Someone puts some coins in the jukebox. *Cocaine* starts playing, filling the café with the sound of Eric Clapton's voice.

This is horrible, my father says, leaving his salad untouched. Cigarettes and now this barbaric music? Let's go.

I still have half an hour before my French class, I tell him, attacking my *steak-frites*. And we were supposed to talk.

Yes, I know . . .

It's for my history project . . .

Yes, yes I know. You want to know about the war. But why here? Why in such a place? Why not at home?

I don't know . . . I guess I wanted to do it somewhere different,

where we wouldn't be interrupted.
My father sniggers. Wouldn't be interrupted. And this place is calmer, hmmm?
He looks at me from behind his glasses and peers at me closely. There's something blue and shiny on your eyelids. What is that?
I sigh, exasperatedly. It's eyeshadow. I'm fifteen years old, aba. Yes, I'm wearing a tiny bit of eye make-up.
He looks floored. And he doesn't know half the truth.
About the bright red lipstick I apply on the street. The fishnet stockings underneath my trousers. The mini skirt shoved into my school bag. The cigarettes zipped inside my pocket. The chewing gum to hide the smell. The boyfriend I kiss in the school hallway and fondle in his house when his father is away. The green hair I had to chop off the other night because the dye wouldn't come off. The music I stash underneath my bed. Telephone, a French band. The Clash, the Pretenders, the Cure, Pink Floyd. And others, too: Joni Mitchell, the Rolling Stones, Neil Young. I listen to them at night, when everyone is sleeping. Forbidden music, this is. So I make up the rules.

So, what do you want to know?
Czernowitz. Start with Czernowitz.
He pours himself a glass of water.
We arrived in Czernowitz in 1940, from Radautz.
Where?
Bukovina. The Austro-Hungarian Empire. We had to flee when it was annexed by the Germans. My father was a communist Jew. A Zionist. Not a good combination for the Germans

although the Soviets didn't mind. They provided us with the house in Czernowitz.

Do you remember it? Czernowitz, I mean?

Of course. It was an intellectual town. A sophisticated place. We lived in a villa. A nice house.

So, your parents were rich?

My father smiles. My mother was a bourgeoise. She came from a prominent family. Before meeting my father, she had fallen for an umbrella manufacturer, a rich man from Bucharest. Her parents were delighted. Then she met my father, a penniless intellectual who spoke ten languages. She chose to marry him instead. My grandparents strongly disapproved. They said that Karl was too intellectual. That he was teaching me the wrong values. That knowledge wasn't essential, but earning a living was.

And what about your father's family?

My father pauses. He had two brothers. One of them had the biggest pharmacy in Czernowitz. He was a respected man. One day he was deported. The Russians said it was because he was a *koulak*. That meant he was exploiting others. My father went to the NKVD to try to save him.

I've been a communist since 1912, Karl said. Please let my brother go.

But the men at the NKVD told him that if he insisted they would send him away too, just like his brother.

What was the NKVD?

The secret service. It became the KGB.

We later found out that my uncle killed himself together with his wife, in the Gulag. They left behind a little girl of four, who was adopted by a family in Russia. She knows nothing of her

past. Nothing about her Jewish roots. Nothing about us.
Did anyone ever try locating her?
My father shakes his head. No. Not that I know of.

I try to picture what the little girl might have looked like. Where she might be living today.
I picture her children. They live in Vladivostok. Or perhaps further west, in the Ukraine. They don't know about their ancestors. About their cousins in Paris.
Or perhaps this woman had no children and died a long time ago, somewhere in a little town near Kirov.
This woman, my cousin.

And the other brother? What about him?
He moved to America. He opened a souvenir shop on Broadway, in New York.
Did he? How come I never met him?
He died. He had no children.

The conversation turns to my father's violin lessons.
I still remember my teacher, he says. A large man who played the double bass in the local orchestra. *Eins zweiE*, he would repeat, over and over again,
Eins zweiE.

Then, there were the lessons his own father drummed into him. Lessons day in, day out. The *Iliad*, Chinese history, French and Italian painting. The story of Napoleon, which developed into a lifelong passion. A stamp collection, which became his pride and joy.

The son was to become what the father had never been.

You must learn.
No play.
Learn.
No play.

Too many lessons, perhaps?
No. Certainly not. There's no such thing as too many lessons.
If you say so.
What do you mean?
Nothing. Go on.

My father covers his ears. Uncovers them. Covers them again. The jukebox is now playing, *'You ain't nothing but a hound dog . . .'*
This is driving me crazy, he mutters. How can my own daughter like such horrible noise?
What kind of music did you listen to at home? I ask, attempting to divert the conversation.
There is only one kind of music, he retorts.
I sigh. What about your violin?
I left it behind with my stamp collection, in Radautz, when we had to flee.

Time hangs somewhere between his words and the bustle around us. Between the sky above our heads and the untouched salad leaves on my father's plate. Between what was then, and what is now. The man at the next table holding his white espresso cup. The Elvis Presley song. The town of Czernowitz in 1941. The violin and the stamp collection my father left behind. My teenage preoccupations. My great-uncle the pharmacist. The electric-blue eyeshadow I bought the other day, at the Monoprix supermarket make-up counter.

I am aware of the disparity between my father's memory and my reality. About adapting history to actuality. About keeping one's balance without falling back into the trap of pain. Because that is, ultimately, what it's about. The ability to let pain ease into endurance.

A boy I know from school comes and sits a few chairs away from me. His name is Olivier. He wears a bandanna around his neck and cowboy boots. I have a faint crush on him, especially since I heard him play the guitar at a school party.
Suddenly, I'm embarrassed to be seen here with my father.

I went to Soviet school, my father continues, ignoring my flustered cheeks.
High School no 5, it was called. We read the *Pravda* newspaper and studied it for one hour every morning. He pauses. Are you listening? You look distracted.
Yes, yes of course I'm listening.
We were given a picture of Stalin which we were meant to hang above our bed. But a colonel in the Russian army, a friend of my father's, told me not to hang the portrait. Read this instead, he said, giving me the Apocalypse of St John. Don't listen to the authorities.
He took a big risk, this man. But he knew, and we knew, that something was wrong. That the world outside was beginning

June 9, 2018

Dear Robert,

Here is a copy of my book, hope you enjoy it - lovely to see you the other evening!

Love Alse

to disintegrate. He told us to come with him to Russia. There's a train tomorrow morning, he said. Come with me. This is your chance to flee.

The Jews must unite, my father answered. We're staying.

So the Russian commissar went alone. His train was bombed and he died in the wreck.

My father munches on a salad leaf and places his fork and knife lengthwise on the plate. I can't eat this.

I shrug my shoulders.

He clears his throat.

I excelled at school, especially at art. The authorities decided to send me to art school in Moscow. But I fell ill with scarlet fever. By the time I recovered, Germany had invaded the USSR.

He pauses. Had I not fallen ill with scarlet fever, I would have become a Russian painter.

The waiter brings my father the bill. We'll continue this conversation at home, he says.

He touches the crown of my head. I remember something else, he says.

Yes?

There was a shop on the Herrengasse in Czernowitz, called Pozudik. We bought ham there. And Suchard chocolate. And many other things. It was an elegant street, the Herrengasse. A bit like the Rue du Faubourg St Honoré.

It sounds nice.

I'm going home now.

Goodbye, aba.

He walks away, slowly.

As I gather my school bag, I can hear Mick Jagger singing

'Angie' on the café jukebox. Olivier is no longer alone. A girl I've never seen before is sitting in front of him. She tosses her red hair back as she speaks to him.

I think of my grandmother and grandfather, whom I never knew. Of my father as a young boy, and the Suchard chocolate inside the Pozudik shop.

I could have been a Russian citizen. I could have been called Natasha, like the heroine in *War and Peace*. I could have lived in Moscow today and listened to Russian rock music. I could have bought jeans on the black market and celebrated New Year's Eve 1981 with a boyfriend who resembled a young Vladimir Mayakovsky.
My futurist-poet hero.

I could have been many things which I am not.
When I know my father to be out of sight, I unzip my pocket and pull a red Marlboro cigarette out of its packet.
I stop to light it by a tree. The sun shines a yellow streak on its leaves. Below my feet, a fleeting shadow.
My own.

2

Two photographs stand on the corner of my father's overflowing bookshelf.
One shows him as a child, with his father and sister, on a visit

to the Herrengasse in Czernowitz, in 1932. It is winter, and all three of them are wearing fur coats and hats.

The other photograph is a family portrait taken in 1939. My grandfather, Karl, has an angular face and stern eyes. He stands behind his wife in a white shirt, dark suit and tie. Pepi sits demurely, her hands neatly crossed on her lap. A brooch is pinned on to her dark dress and her hair is neatly combed back. Elena stands on her left, in a neat white frock, her long hair parted on the side. She is fifteen years old, and smiles widely at the camera.

My father, who is ten but appears much younger, stands between his parents, dressed in flannel Bermuda shorts, a white shirt and tie, and a single-breasted lapel jacket with three gold buttons. He wears round glasses and seems pensive.

There is an atmosphere of quiet formality in the photograph. It is visible in their overall demeanour, but also in the family backdrop (a framed photograph hanging on a wall – their wall? – the plush, ottoman-style armchair my grandmother is sitting in). What did the photographer see as he snapped their picture? I wonder. Did he notice the stiff body language between Pepi and her husband? The carefree attitude in Elena's gestures? Did he discern a gifted child behind my father's thick frames? Perhaps he only focused on their gaze. On their spotless attire. Their attire, that day.

I can almost smell the soap they would have used before changing into their finest clothes. The French perfume my grandmother would have dabbed on her wrists. The hair gel Elena would have passed through her wavy hair. The polish Karl would have used on his shoes.

The photographer couldn't possibly know that within two years, those same people he had photographed would be covered in filth and infested with lice. That they would contract typhus in a Romanian concentration camp.
That they would fight for their lives in sub-zero temperatures, and that their feet would turn to ice.
That they, along with many others, would be stripped of their humanity but would keep their indignity to themselves. Because once indignity is unleashed, there is no turning back.

You must be strong and resilient.
You cannot fall.

3

Pepi had three brothers. One of them, Dori, lived in a palatial villa in Bucharest. When Elena turned sixteen, Dori gave a ball for her.
Dori Korn, like his brothers, was a rich industrialist. An arms manufacturer, he provided sabres for the Romanian army and was said to have connections in high places. In the 1930s, Dori and his wife left for a trip around the world. He sent postcards from far-flung continents. The stamps were duly placed inside my father's stamp collection.
When the war broke out, Dori's connections helped him out of Romania and into Palestine. His brothers followed his example. Isio left for Italy. Manfred for America. Josi for Brazil. Pepi didn't make it out of the country, because she was married to Karl.

Who, after all, would want to extend privileges to a man such as Karl? He was said to be a member of a Zionist communist organisation. When the Russo-Finnish war broke out, he proclaimed that his heart was with the Finns but his head with the Russians.
He had given up accountancy to dabble in chemistry and essential oils.
Essential oils?

Josi settled in São Paulo. He started his own investment bank and married Lucia. Together they had two daughters, Rafaella and Anna. Anna is three years older than me. She moved to Paris when she turned eighteen. She studied history of art at the École du Louvre, then disappeared.
What does she look like?

Like this.
Dark, wavy long hair, thick lips, brown eyes, almond-shaped just like her father's. Tall and athletic, she has an easy-going self-confidence which stems from her upbringing and the fact that she has never wanted for anything. Nothing like me. Or my family. There is nothing easy about my upbringing and I want for everything. All the time. Not because my parents are poor but because everything around me seems more appealing than what I have.
Josi and Lucia Korn were different from us. So different, that they never attempted to contact my father, and vice versa.
I have nothing to say to these bourgeois people, my father said. What do they know about painting? About music?
It's not about them, darling, my mother answered quietly. It's

about their daughter. It would be nice for the girls to meet her. She is a cousin, after all.

My mother tried to find Anna. She called Pepi who claimed that she had lost touch with Josi many years before. He didn't behave well with me, she said. He forgot about me when he married that awful woman.

I looked through the phone book and called directory enquiries. Nothing.

A few times, I went to the École du Louvre and stood outside its front door, hoping to see a darker version of myself. A stream of fashionable students passed by, but no one who could have been Anna Korn. Or at least, no one who corresponded to the vision I had of Anna Korn.

When I went to the admissions office and asked for her I was told by a stern-looking woman, her grey hair tied in a tight bun, that they didn't give out that sort of information. That personal details were called personal for a reason.

So, eventually, I gave up.

I imagine Anna in Paris. She lives in the Marais district, on the Rue de Sevigné.

She complains about the Parisian weather and misses her native land. Yet, she has grown attached to Paris. Her family comes and visits a few times. Josi offers to buy her a larger apartment.

She refuses.

Stubborn girl, he says.

At night, Anna gets dressed up and goes to nightclubs. She has affairs with various men and falls in love with a Lebanese caterer, Youssef. He has green eyes and dark skin. He comes from Beirut and cooks dinners for her in his apartment on the Rue des Martyrs.

Anna is smitten. Her parents are not.

He's not the man for you, Josi says.

But I love him, she tells her father.

I don't, he retorts.

They eventually separate. She drowns her sorrows at the Bains Douches nightclub. We could have met there. We could have danced side by side, Anna with her long dark hair and perfectly toned figure, me with my thick curly hair and gangly legs.

We could have danced to Grace Jones and the Talking Heads and Serge Gainsbourg. We might have exchanged a few words, or perhaps she might have asked me for a cigarette. And as she blew the smoke away, it would have been impossible for us to know that we shared a gene pool. That our common lineage stretched far away from the booming music and spotlights of the Bains Douches, all the way to the streets of Bukovina, before the German tanks rolled in.

4

You want to know more?
Yes.
All right.
I'm listening.
Not now. Henri and Martine are coming for tea. We'll talk about it after they leave.

We are sitting in the living room, surrounded by books and drawings. It is a winter afternoon.
The phone rings.
I pick it up. It's Susanna, an eccentric and beautiful art critic from New York, whom Noga and I have known since birth. She was once married to a famous American pop artist. After a string of lovers she married a music producer. The producer eventually took to drinking and Susanna became a compulsive shopper.

In her spare time, Susanna writes influential books and articles on the state of the art world. She lives between Paris and New York, where her keen real-estate eye has ensured her a steady income.

Just in case.

Her children are both at boarding school and call their mother by her first name when she pays them an occasional visit.

Susanna's daughter, Tracy, is a friend of mine. Three years older than me, she's the most independent girl I know. When not at boarding school, she lives with her father, the pop artist, in a large Manhattan loft which he shares with his new wife and children.

Tracy came to stay with us in Paris, a few months ago. She was fifteen years old but looked eighteen. She bought me a Donna Summers record and we played it in my bedroom. When my father heard the music he was horrified.

How can you listen to such barbaric garbage? he asked.

Tracy laughed.

I shuddered.

Your father should see what happens in the school dorms, she smirked. He'd have a ball . . .

What happens?

She looked at me. All kinds of things. You don't want to know, trust me.

But I do!

All right. I'll give you the edited version. I don't want to get into trouble with your parents.

Why would my parents find out?

Why indeed . . .

She told me about her various boyfriends at boarding school. About sex and drugs. About the rivalry between some of her girlfriends. About an older man she knew in New York. We've been having a secret affair, she said.

I was both shocked and impressed. But I pretended to feel neither.

Tracy wore lipstick, torn jeans, and smoked a cigarette on my balcony.

I would never have dared.

Did her mother know what her daughter was up to? I wondered. Would she have even cared?

Come over for dinner tomorrow, my father says to Susanna. And don't be late, he adds.

Susanna is never punctual.

I will be going to New York this summer, on my own. I will stay with Tracy and the Manns, musician friends of my parents. They said they would look after me.
My parents are thinking about it.

Yes.
Please, yes.

5

My father comes from a faraway place.
I cannot see it or explain it, but I can feel it. In that place, there are words for things which no longer exist.
Somehow, traces of it have managed to seep into my consciousness. It has contributed to the foundation of me, like mortar in an unfinished building.
I can almost taste the atmosphere on the tip of my tongue.
When my father goes, that atmosphere will disappear with him.
Will its residue disappear with me?
When will the building of me be whole?
I wonder if one ever knows.

6

My parents fight at night. I cannot hear what my father says to my mother, but I can feel her tremble, almost as if I were standing in the room, with her.
His voice is loud and booming. Hers is subdued and barely audible. Stop it! I can hear her tell him in hurried whispers. You'll wake the girls up.
He shouts again. Then, a loud noise, like a door slamming.
I hide my head under the pillow.
I don't want to know.

7

The photographer Henri Cartier-Bresson has piercing blue eyes and a childish laugh; it is hard not to warm to him. Henri proclaims himself an anarchist and says that he likes to sleep on the floor. He has travelled throughout the world and often speaks of his encounters. The people he knew, and those he didn't. The faces that inspired him. I never knew when I was going to take a picture, he said. It's not about knowing, but seeing.

I once told my father that Henri's photographs spoke to me in a way that Sam's plays did not.
That's because you're too young to understand, my father said. To me, the power of beauty is not about reason. It is about emotion and truth.
My father's truth isn't mine.

Nor is my truth anyone else's, although I would like it to be. Sometimes.

Noga and I sit down with Henri and Martine. We drink tea and eat chocolate biscuits.
Last summer, we spent a few days in their Luberon country house. Various people came and went. Painters, writers, and an elegant woman who lived in New York. Dinner was served outdoors. We watched the sun set over the Alpilles mountains.
The adults drank wine and spoke about painting and politics. About Buddhism and India.
The next morning, we went for a walk in the hills. Martine and I spoke about school. She had a gentle manner about her which made me feel secure.

There is a lot to be said for gentle manners.

I venture some thoughts on photography. Henri listens. I like photography. Kertesz. Capa. Brassai. Izis. And of course, him, Henri. But I certainly won't tell him that.
My father admonishes me. How many times do I have to tell you not to interrupt us?
I get up and leave the room.
Come back! I am told.
I don't.

Later, my father takes me aside.
Did you hear us fight last night? he asks.
I nod.

I lost my temper, he says. I'm very sorry. Your mother drives me so crazy sometimes that I don't know what to do . . .
He looks disconsolate, as if his face were about to melt into a puddle of grief.
I won't shout again, he promises.

8

My father paces around the living room. Henri and Martine have left. My mother has had to run to an appointment and Noga is doing her homework.

I'll tell you about 1941, my father says.
I'm listening.

In October 1941, the Jews of Czernowitz were asked to assemble in the town square. Bring one suitcase per person, they were told.
My mother, sister and I packed a few necessities. Karl, instead, placed thirty bottles of essential oils inside a beautiful black leather attaché case.
I could barely contain my excitement. Where are we going? I kept asking. Are we going on a trip? I had just turned twelve.
My father pauses. Can you imagine that I was excited about such a thing?
No. Yes. No. Go on.

The Romanian and German soldiers were dressed in *Reithosen*.

Riding trousers. They herded us into a cattle wagon. Those who protested were beaten-up.
The doors closed on us. There were between eighty and a hundred of us per wagon. We couldn't tell the difference between day and night.
We were moving east, we were told. Always east.
The wagons eventually stopped somewhere between the Dniester and Bug Rivers, in the Ukraine. For days on end, we were made to walk through mud and sleet and snow. The season hardened, and so did the earth below our feet. By the time we arrived in Luchinetz, in Bessarabia, the temperature had dropped to minus forty degrees. The coldest winter of the century.
We lived in a miserable hut in the market square, together with Mrs Feinstein. Once an elegant woman who had held a weekly salon in Czernowitz, she was now covered in lice, as we were. She had a son called Nyousha, who became my friend. Nyousha taught me how to chop wood. How to build muscle tone.

One morning, we were rounded up by Romanian soldiers and told that we were moving east again. That we were leaving immediately.
My father protested. Do you have a warrant?
A soldier approached him and let out a stream of invective. So my father slapped him with the back of a gloved hand.
He had gloves?
Yes. He had gloves.
And then?
He was beaten up, and, together with some two thousand of

us, was then marched out of the village into the glacial wind. The Russians called it the *Zaverucka* wind.
Some cried. We walked. My father with difficulty. He was in pain.
At one point, as we were passing by a ravine, I felt a kick. I looked up, quickly, to see my father had kicked me off the slope. My parents and sister tumbled down after me.
We landed in the dense, snow-filled Ukrainian forest.
And then?
My father looks at his watch. I have to go.
Now?
Yes. I have an appointment at the Louvre at three o'clock.
But that's in an hour!
Don't tell me what to do. I need to prepare myself. I'm never late for appointments. I'm not a teenager like you –
OK, OK . . .
They need me to identify a Raphael painting.
A Raphael painting?
Yes. A taxi driver from Strasbourg found it in his mother's attic. It could be a fake. Or a real one. One never knows.
I fidget with my hair. But what happened after you rolled down the hill?
I'll tell you another day.

He gets up and leaves me sitting in the living room, together with the empty teacups and chocolate-biscuit crumbs. Together with the convoy of refugees and Karl's gloved hand. Together with the snow-filled forest and unidentified Raphael painting. Together with the sound of his footsteps as he walks away.

9

In a book entitled *History of the Jews of Bukovina*, I read this extract about my great-uncle, the pharmacist:

> *Pharmacist Dlugacz, a joyful man, couldn't understand how the strange cold world could be so terribly cruel as to repay the goodness of him and his family with evil. His exterior mirrored his inner nature. He was always clean and elegant and never carelessly dressed because he viewed that as an insult to his surroundings. When it came to arranging large functions, friend Dlugacz was always there. He worked happily to help others. And this gregarious, helpful man was swallowed by the wide icy Siberian earth.*

10

We go to a concert, at the Théâtre des Champs Elysées. The programme is Beethoven, Ligeti and Schubert. As soon as the music begins, my father emits grunts and groans. I cringe and quiver in my seat. I cannot think of anything more embarrassing than my father's musical antics. From afar, he looks as if he were praying towards Mecca, his head swinging back and forth in synchronicity with his hands.
But then, I give into the music and I forget.

I lose myself in a Schubert string quartet. *Death and the Maiden.* I close my eyes and the notes dance in front of me like black and white figures. I can feel their pulsating beat rushing through my bloodstream. They swerve and glide and slide and then, no more.

The end.

Ripping, roaring applause. My father stands up, visibly shaken.

Wasn't it beautiful? My mother asks me.

It was all right, I answer, shrugging my shoulders for maximum effect.

V

August in Manhattan.

I have spent three weeks travelling with a family from Wisconsin. They drop me off in Manhattan, after a drive through the Midwest.

I am staying with Edward and Monica Mann, who live in a sprawling apartment on Central Park West.

Monica has immaculately coiffed, pitch-black hair. She has a sweet manner and a slight Spanish accent when she speaks.

Edward, a renowned concert pianist, wears black patent-leather shoes and tailored shirts. He practises several hours a day on an imposing grand piano which stands in the living room.

The Mann penthouse apartment has a sprawling view of the Manhattan skyline. The skyscrapers seem pasted against the blue sky. Their stillness vibrates.

In the distance, the sun rests atop the Empire State Building, like a golden crown.

I have never seen such architectural freedom before. There is an uncanny order to this modern steel chaos. Do the inhabitants resemble their landscape? I wonder, as I stare out of the window.

Edward twirls his whiskey on the rocks. He asks me about my trip and my parents. I answer politely, unable to detach my eyes from the view outside their large glass window.

Monica asks me if I'd like a sandwich and a glass of milk.

I shudder. I'm thirteen years old, I tell her.
I know, she replies, sounding confused.
I don't drink milk any more, I explain.
I see.

She shows me to my bedroom. It smells good, like fresh apples. She explains that as Edward is practising for his up-coming concert, I shouldn't, under any circumstances, bother him or talk to him during the day.
And dinner is at six o'clock, she adds, leaving me to unpack.
Six o'clock?

The Manns have no children and it shows.
I feel ill at ease with them, and although Monica tries her best, Edward has a rough manner with me.
Dinner is cold food. Bagels, sandwiches, salmon. I pick at my food and make a meagre attempt at conversation.

The next morning, as we sit down for breakfast, I notice margarine on the table. Do you have any butter? I ask.
No. Sweet 'n' Low, margarine, but no butter.
How can you eat such poison? I ask them, pointing towards the margarine pack.

Monica and Edward look at me in shock horror.
And say nothing.

The next day, after I make another inappropriate comment, Edward slaps me hard across the face.
Arrogant girl, he says.

I've never been slapped before.
I rush to my bedroom and throw myself on the bed, in tears.
Teenagers are like flies, my father says. Can't get rid of their annoying buzz.
Am I like a fly?
I must leave this place.
I must.

I finally emerge from the bedroom with teary eyes.
I'd like to call my parents, I tell Monica.
She points towards the telephone.
My father answers.
I know better than to ask him.
Can I speak to mummy?
She's at a lecture. What is it?
I want to go and stay with Tracy, I whisper.
Want? Is this about 'want'? Tracy's a terrible influence on you, my father says. And she listens to that horrible music of yours –
Please. Just for a few nights. I can't stay here any more . . .
OK, he grumbles. I'll talk to your mother about it and we'll call you later.

The next morning, Susanna comes to pick me up.
She wears a turban around her head and bright red lipstick. Her green eyes sparkle in the light and her dimpled smile is a welcome respite from the stifling atmosphere at the Manns.
The Manns greet her warmly. I'm now in charge of this young woman, Susanna smiles.
Edward looks visibly relieved.

Monica kisses me goodbye and wishes me luck. She hands me my suitcase and closes the door gently behind me.

We stand by the elevator and Susanna looks at me. No wonder you were freaking out in there . . .
Freaking out? I'm not sure what she means but I pretend that I do.
I know, I say gravely.
She looks at me strangely.
We're going to drop off this suitcase of yours at my place, and then we're going shopping, she says, looking at me from top to toe.
You need some make-up. And some clothes. After that, I'll drop you off at Tracy's.

We take a taxi to her house, on East 57th Street. Susanna hands my suitcase to a white-gloved doorman and we drive off to Bergdorf Goodman. We walk through the perfume department where women dressed in short skirts stand in corners holding sprays in their hands. Would you like to smell the new Nina Ricci perfume? They ask.
I would.
But Susanna doesn't.

We pick a black kohl pencil and lipstick.
Let's put it on now, she says.
We stand by a mirror. I've worn eyeliner before, you know, I tell her, applying a black line inside and above my lid.
Well, thank God for that, she replies, tartly.

We walk out carrying several shopping bags. Susanna bought

herself some clothes.
Many clothes.

It is hot and muggy outside. No breeze. No wind.
The mugginess seems to stand still, as if stuck in mid-air.

2

Tracy lives downtown with her father and stepmother, Theresa. It is the first time I have stepped inside a loft, and I'm impressed. The walls are covered with Bob's paintings. Large, colourful half-circles within square borders. A large, three-dimensional metal sculpture. Bits of furniture are strewn around the room, in no particular order.
A young man comes to greet us. Bob's assistant.
Assistant?
Oh yes, Tracy explains, he has many.
My father has no assistants. He stretches his canvases alone and mixes his own pigments. His works are done in one sitting, no retouches allowed. He has invented his own method of printing copper plates, using a brush needle and sugar ink, before winding his etchings through his printing press. Sometimes Noga and I help.
I love the smell of fresh ink.
Seeing an aquatint roll out of the press.

I ask Tracy if she ever helps her father. No, she replies. His assistants do that.

On our way to Tracy's bedroom we meet Bob and Theresa. A

cigar stump is stuck between his lips.
Hi, he says, shaking my hand. Last time I saw you, you were an infant . . .
I'm not sure what my reaction is meant to be.
Oh, I answer, placidly.
How's your father doing?
Fine. He's fine.
This is Theresa, he says, introducing his wife.
Her hair is stuck in a clumsy bun and her glasses are slipping off her nose. She looks harried.
We're going to my bedroom, Tracy states firmly.
Are you staying for dinner? Theresa calls out as we're walking away.
Don't know, Tracy grumbles and looks at me. Theresa's a bitch, she says. I hate her.

Should I hate her too?

Tracy's clothes are strewn across her bedroom. She climbs across a stack of sweaters and reaches for a record. The Rolling Stones, followed by Dr John and Joni Mitchell. She puts the records on high volume.
This is really cool stuff, she says.
I nod in agreement.
We're going out, she declares, after a short while. Gotta meet one of my friends who's in trouble.
Trouble?
Yeah, like you know, drugs kinda thing.
Oh sure, sure.

I wonder what the Manns would say if I were to show up at

their doorstep again.
They would probably kick me out.
Maybe I should go back to Paris instead.

I'm hungry. I'm tired. I want to go home.

We eat a hamburger and fries on Prince Street. Later, we meet Tracy's friend Jeff, by the Hudson River. He has long blond hair and his eyes look glassy. Tracy talks to him briefly. He lights a cigarette and walks away, dragging his feet behind him.

I'm not sure what happened between them. Did she give him money? Did he give her drugs?

I think he just wanted company, she says. He's pretty stoned. A rich-kid druggie is what he is. He's not used to being alone.

I don't know what to say.

Men walk past us, dressed in tight jeans and sleeveless white T-shirts.
Music is blaring from a boom box, a mixture of fast-talking and heavy beats.

> *. . . The rock it to the bang-bang boogie say up jumped the boogie to the rhythm of the boogie the beat . . .*

You hear the beat? It's called hip-hop, Tracy explains.
A crowd of people starts to dance.
I stare, mesmerised.

I feel like joining in.

Some of these guys are transsexuals, Tracy tells me, pointing towards the dancers. And gay prostitutes. And mega drug addicts. And kids just like you and me.
I don't like being called a kid.
How come Tracy doesn't seem to mind?
She looks at me and laughs.
I think you should come to New York more often, she declares, lighting a cigarette and blowing the smoke towards the river.

Perhaps.
Or perhaps not.

3

My mother and I step off the crowded 21 bus and walk towards the Boulevard Haussmann. We push the revolving door of the Galeries Lafayette open and head for the escalators.
I'm sure you'll find what you need here, my mother says.
We never find anything here, I mutter. It's so uncool.
Well, maybe this time you'll be surprised.

We stop on the second floor and walk through the clothes department.
The young and adult section.
My mother stops in front of various dresses. A duffle coat. A ruffled shirt. A plaid skirt.
I abhor plaid skirts. And ruffled shirts.

Look at this, she says, pointing at a Laura Ashley flowing skirt.
I think it's lovely.
Not for me, I mumble.
I set my sights on a black designer coat. Knee length with large leather buttons.
Too expensive, my mother says.
A pair of black trousers.
If you like them, she sighs.

I do.

I find my size on a rack and try them on in the fitting room.
I stand a few feet back and look at myself in the floor length mirror.
They fit perfectly.

She's very thin, I hear a saleswoman tell my mother.
I know, my mother sighs.
Too thin, the saleswoman adds.
My father was very tall and thin, just like her, my mother says.
I understand. What do you think about the trousers, young lady? the saleswoman asks me. She's short, with an impatient face and an uneven smile.
I like them, I mumble.
(I hate being called 'young lady'.)

We need a coat too, my mother declares firmly.
Of course, madame, the saleswoman replies, obligingly. What kind of coat are you looking for?
Thank you but I can look for it on my own, I answer, casting a furious glance at my mother.

I think we'll be OK, she mutters reluctantly.
I understand, the saleswoman replies. You can pay for the trousers at the cashier over there, she adds, pointing towards the back of the department.
Thank you, I say, running off.
What about your coat? My mother shouts, trailing behind me.
Forget the coat. I don't want a coat.
But it's cold outside.
I don't want a coat, I repeat. Not here. I hate this shop. I'll buy it in the flea market.
The flea market. Always the flea market, she mumbles.

I pass the shoe department on my way to the cashier. My eyes fall upon a pair of short, black suede boots, with a pointy toe. My dream shoes.
I stop and glance at them carefully. I take them in my hands, pressing the soft suede fabric between my fingers. I bring them towards my nose and inhale them deeply.
I love these, I tell my mother.
We're not here for shoes. You've got enough shoes. We're here for a coat, trousers, a shirt, anything but shoes.
I plead with her. But she doesn't budge.
Clothes, yes. Shoes, no. If we buy you these you won't get a winter coat.
I told you, I don't want a coat! I shout.
This is not about what you want but what you need! She shouts back.

We start arguing. My tone escalates.
Don't you dare raise your voice to me, she snaps.

Fine.
I clutch my trousers and walk away angrily. Past a row of neatly folded jumpers and evening wear. Past the coat and children's departments. Past the designer gowns and ladies lingerie. I glance at a mannequin in matching silk pink bra and underwear, a suspender belt clipped to her dark stockings.
It makes me squirm.

I run down an escalator, then up again.
Somehow, I end up at the opposite end of the shop.
I stop in my tracks.
I have lost my mother.
I walk quickly past the evening-wear department. Silken dresses and sequin blouses hold court with tulle and velvet gowns worn by faceless mannequins.
I accelerate my pace towards the stockings department.
A woman walks past me, leaving behind a trail of perfume. I know that smell. Shalimar?
An elderly woman wearing a fur coat grabs a few tights in her hand and runs her polished nail through a silk pair on display.
How many denier? she asks the saleswoman.
Thirty, madame, replies the saleswoman.

I look down, towards the floor below me. At the large, spiral staircase.
I feel dizzy. My neck feels constricted, as if I were choking.
I'm hot.
Very hot.
Soon, I shall faint.
Unless I find my mother.

My infuriating mother.
How do I find her?
I cannot possibly page her. Not at fifteen years old.
What if I bump into somebody I know from school?
Too risky.
Must find her on my own.

I run back up the escalator and start to search for her frantically. Back where we left off. Near the shoes. The skirts. The trousers. The fitting rooms.
Ah, the fitting rooms. Same saleswoman, except that this time she's taking care of another family. A rich family.
The daughter, about my age, prances around in an expensive dress. I noticed that dress before. Agnès B. White and red dots with a round collar.
Six hundred francs. Beyond my wildest dreams.

Cette robe est très jolie, Ondine, the mother declares in a clipped tone. Her words sound as if they have been scrubbed clean. Diamond earrings sparkle in her lobes and her eyes are heavily made-up. She wears a deep-red trouser suit and high heels. She looks like Sophie's mother.

You're right, madame, this is a lovely dress, the saleswoman affirms. Very popular with the young people.
Young Ondine wears a golden cross around her neck and a shiny bangle on her wrist.
I love it, she says. Let's buy it.
Fine. Would you please wrap this up, the mother tells the saleswoman, with a hint of condescension in her tone. And

now, Ondine, why don't you try on those other clothes you like, I don't have all day . . .

Fine.
Fine? Just like that?
No doubt. No guilt. No putting it aside for the next day. No thinking about it. No, yes I really love it, please buy it for me and I promise I won't ask for anything ever again.

I stand transfixed. Does Ondine always get what she wants?

Everything all right, mademoiselle? The saleswoman asks me, with that same unnerving smile.
Oh yes, fine, thank you, fine.

I walk away rapidly.
Where is my mother?
I am about to faint.
My legs feel wobbly.
I can feel the heat rising, from my toes to my neck.
I will be carried out on a stretcher into Boulevard Haussmann, and the local hospital will inject me with adrenalin. Just like they did with Brigitte in the school cafeteria, when she had an allergic reaction to eggs.

Oh, there you are! I hear a voice exclaim behind me.
I turn around swiftly.
My mother.
A short figure with curly black hair, hazel eyes and a worried face.

I've been looking for you, she says.
I sigh deeply. And I for you.

No more neck constriction. Or heat rising. Or wobbly legs.
Will you buy me these shoes, mummy? I ask, plaintively, pointing towards the ankle boots.
She shakes her head.
No. And don't ask me again.

I don't then.
But I do later.
Again, and again.
She doesn't relent.

VI

It is Yom Kippur. The Day of Atonement. We follow my mother to the synagogue on the Rue Copernic. My father stays behind.
Not for me, he says. You go.
We don't want to go! my sister and I exclaim.
Follow your mother and don't argue with me.
My father doesn't believe in anything. Why should we, then? It's not fair.
This is not about fairness but duty, he answers firmly.

We sit upstairs, among a crowded row of women and children. The Rabbi sings in his monotonous voice, while the congregation stands up. And sits down. And stands up again. There is something mechanical about the habits of prayer. The Rabbi's repetitive drone obliterates the spiritual intent. At least for me it does. And for the others?
I look around me. The men on our left wear dark suits and white tallit scarves wrapped around their shoulders. They sway their bodies to and fro, in synchronised rhythm, like ticking pendulums.
Near me, a plump woman wearing a red hat cries softly. A little boy tugs at his mother's sleeve. A young girl wearing gloves looks lost in thought. She's very pretty. Neat, well dressed, sitting demurely. A tall, attractive woman, presumably her mother, sits near her. She wears an impeccably tailored suit, an expensive necklace around her neck. I look at her. At the sense of entitlement which she projects.

I wonder about the young girl, probably my age. Fifteen years old.
She must live with her mother and banker father in the 16th arrondissement, in a large apartment with parquet floors and expensive rugs. She has two brothers whom she bickers with but adores. David and Raphael. Or perhaps Edouard and Cyril. Or even better, Alexandre et Charles.
The girl is called Myriam. Without a doubt.
There is, of course, a housekeeper who's been around since Myriam's birth.
The family has a house in St Tropez, which they use in the summer. In the winter, they go to Crans-sur-Sierre, in Switzerland.
They swim, they ride, they ski, they drive.
My family does none of the above.

My mother nudges me. Keep still, she says. Now comes the important part.
We press our fists against our chests to ask for repentance. Sins committed, sins forgiven.
What sins have I committed?
My mother has no sense of entitlement. She rarely wears tailored suits and doesn't own expensive necklaces. We have some help but no staff, and most of our holidays tend to be close to main roads. No such thing as driving into the wilderness. Or to unknown continents. We stick to what we know. And what we know is without a car.

My mother is good and gentle. Patient and kind.
And I hate her for it.

I lie. I scream. I shout at my parents. I resent their purity and knowledge. Their values and morals.
My father's anger. My mother's goodness.
But I cannot detach myself from them. I try, but cannot remove myself from the gene pool which has determined my emotional miasma. I can only vent my anger in front of my family. No one else.
My safe and sound audience.

I yearn for stolidity but find that I don't even know where to begin.
How does one appear nonchalant? Impassive?
How does one hold back?

My father never holds back and thinks nonchalance is a bourgeois concept.

Your family is so different, my friend Sophie once told me. It must be so amazing to live in that kind of atmosphere.
Amazing? No, I say. It's not.
But you don't know how lucky you are! I wish I had such a family. My parents are so boring . . .
They're not boring, I say, thinking about Sophie's parents. Her father, a small man with round glasses, is an advertising mogul. Her mother is a graceful woman with long legs and a young face. She dresses in Chanel and always says the right things.
How does she do it?
I never seem to get it right. My gestures are clumsy and my timing is poor. I know little about appropriate reflexes. About charm and pretence.

Anyway, charm is worthless compared to knowledge, as my father would say.
My cultural gaps are endless. You're so ignorant, I am often told.
Stupid girl. Why don't you ever listen to me? Why don't you learn from me?

Because I don't want to listen.
Because my father preaches when he speaks.
Because he expects me to know everything when I clearly know nothing.
And nothing is less effort than everything.

I should know. At school, I stare out of the window vacantly. I pretend to pay attention to the teachers when, in reality, I am miles away.
At least I have my piano playing and books to fall back on. And the stories I write, about penniless Russian boys in Moscow who secretly flee their home town and find fortune in the West. Or poor, ragged French villagers who huddle by the fire while their wealthy masters host lavish parties.
I lose myself in books. Stories, novels, memoirs. I am affected unexpectedly, inadvertently. I lose myself in the lives of others.

2

We meet Sam for tea at the Café Français. It is part of the PLM St Jacques, a bland 1970s' hotel on the Boulevard St Jacques, near his home.

It is a strange café in an unfashionable part of Paris, precisely the reason why Sam likes to go there. Named after the Paris-Lyons-Marseilles train, it is moments away from the Prison de la Santé, Paris's most notorious jail. Sam says that on quiet days, he can hear prisoners shouting across the rooftops.

He is waiting for us when we arrive, seated in one of the orange booths. A few Japanese tourists sit at the next table, speaking in quiet voices.

Sam has a brown beret on his head, a cigar between his lips. He looks frailer than usual.

A bit on the tired side, Sam says, when my father enquires about his health.

We discuss the election of François Mitterrand. Sam is pleased about it, and so are my parents.

He'll be all right as long as he doesn't succumb to communist pressure, my father says.

What will a few communists do? Sam retorts. Anyway, the communist intellectuals are all against Georges Marchais. He's no good.

On the night of Mitterrand's election, I stood with thousands of other young people in the Place de la Bastille. We shared his visions and dreams. The abolition of the death penalty. Racial equality. Steady employment. We cried victory and shouted '*On a gagné!*' in the rain. We all walked home that

night, brimming with excitement about the new future that awaited us.
Us, French men and women.
Us, like me.
This was where I belonged.

The conversation veers towards books. I tell Sam about the novels I have just read. Marguerite Duras and Simone de Beauvoir. I love her autobiography, *Memoires d'une jeune fille rangée.*
Why do you love it? Sam asks, his crystal-blue eyes peering at me.
Because it speaks to me. I feel as if I know her.
He smiles. That's good, he says.
He asks me about my fifteenth birthday. I owe you a present, he says.
My father becomes pale. Her birthday was terrible. Barbaric . . .
Not now, my mother interjects.
Why not? Instead of coming to my opening in Dijon, my daughter chose to have a party instead.
My father pauses and breathes in deeply.
I can still smell the spaghetti bolognese that was thrown against the walls of the flat. And I can see those degenerates smoking cigarettes and doing horrible things in the bathtub.
Enough, my mother snaps, Sam doesn't need to hear about this.

Sam smiles, flicks the ashes of his cigar into the ashtray, and says nothing.

3

Marie and Nicolas Barzin ask Noga and me over for tea. You can watch television if you'd like.

The Barzins are confirmed atheists and, to Noga and me, the closest one could get to normality.

They live right next door to us in a large atelier flat, just like ours. Marie's mother, an art dealer who was married to a surrealist, has known my father since the early fifties. The Barzin household is filled with Picabia and de Chirico paintings, and a treasure trove of surrealist papers, which students and academics pore over regularly.

The Barzin children, Simon and Victor, are ten years younger than us and feel like extended family.

Noga and I spend a lot of time in their house. We have no television and the Barzin household is like a technological paradise. Not only do they have a television, but also a VCR, complete with French blockbusters and Hollywood films.

At the weekends, the Barzins spend time in the Loire Valley, in a rambling house which once belonged to Marie's mother.

In the winter, they go skiing. And every summer they visit the Côte d'Azur or far flung destinations, returning with tales about their adventurous escapades.

We are bland in comparison.

We seldom travel and our adventures are purely cerebral.

How come we never explore other countries? I ask my mother.

We go to Israel a lot. Isn't that travelling?

It's boring to go to Israel all the time, No, I mean different

countries, like Spain or Italy or . . . I don't know, the Comoros Islands? (I have a 1975 stamp from there. It features the Anjouan sunbird, with a hooked beak and velvety plumage.)
My mother widens her eyes. The Comoros Islands? Where are they?
North of Madagascar.
Madagascar! What are you going to say next, Timbuktu? We don't travel because we can't afford it. Travelling is expensive. Especially if you want to go to the Indian Ocean . . .
So forget about the Indian Ocean, I answer. Why can't we go somewhere that's not expensive? Like, I don't know, Brittany for example?
Ask your father, my mother sighs. Don't ask me.
I don't want to ask him.
So don't, she retorts.

4

You know the answer, a maths teacher tells me. You just need to think about it harder.

But I don't. How could I? I barely understand his question.
And I don't like to question what I don't understand.
I don't want to reveal my weaknesses.
So the school decides to do it for me instead.

We can no longer keep your daughter here, the headmaster tells my parents. I'm sorry, but we have a reputation to maintain.

A reputation to maintain.

5

A new school in the 15th arrondissement.

I make friends quickly. Another world has opened up for me. The world of best friends, boyfriends and sartorial preoccupations.
I fall in love with dimpled Matthieu and decide to become a punk, just like him. Matthieu has spiked blond hair and wears combat boots.
I follow him to parties on the outskirts of Paris, filled with skinheads with beady eyes and safety pins in their ears.
I'm scared of them.
But I pretend otherwise.

One night, I witness a group of punks and skinheads vandalising a school. They shout and curse as papers and fliers are tossed out of the window into the chill of the night.
I'm cold, I tell Matthieu. I think I want to go home.
You're not cut out to be a punk, he tells me.
We break up soon afterwards.

In my bedroom I fill my diary with poems and songs.

We read one of Sam's plays at school. *Endgame*. It hits an unexpected nerve. I like the combination of austerity and humour. No surplus, all essentials; something to strive for, when I'm older and wiser. Too early, for now.

I write a short story, which I show to my father.

It’s good, he says. You should send it to Sam.
And so begins a correspondence between the two of us. I send him my garbled attempts at poetry and short stories.
If he likes what he sees, Sam writes to me, in his spidery handwriting. Small white note cards, covered in black ink. Some envelopes don’t even bear a stamp, a testament to his habit of walking from his apartment to our letterbox. A fifteen-minute walk.

Sam doesn’t always write back.
And I pay heed to his silences.
Once, I overhear him tell my father that I may become a writer.

I may.

As the years go by, his notes start to fill my desk drawer. And then one day, they disappear. I look frantically for them, to no avail.

Nobody knows.

6

I come back from school one winter evening and hear my parents fighting. I march directly into my bedroom, throw my school bag on to my bed and lie down.
Have they heard me come home?
Noga comes out of her bedroom and walks into mine. She looks upset. They're having a fight, she says. Aba is shouting at mummy.
I know, I can hear them, I say. A lot of parents have fights.

You stupid woman! My father shouts. Stupid, ignorant woman! Just like your mother!
My mother says nothing. Or if she does, we don't hear her.

Noga has tears in her eyes.
What is it? I ask, coldly.
Nothing. It's just . . . Julien, she mumbles before suddenly starting to cry.
What about Julien? I sigh impatiently.
There was a party this afternoon and he wouldn't dance with me. I've never danced with a boy, she adds, tears flowing down her cheeks.
I reach out my hand towards her. I'd like to hug her.
But I find it difficult to do.

I'm leaving you! we suddenly hear my mother shout. I've had enough.
So go! my father barks.

My sister and I remain motionless. Noga seems to have momentarily forgotten about Julien.
My mother walks towards the front door. My father runs after her.
I'm sorry. I'm very sorry, he repeats.
Leave me alone, my mother snaps, trying to push him away.
Please forgive me, he implores her. Don't leave.

I look at him. His face bears the weight of his deeds.
Noga follows me. My mother is getting into the elevator and my father tries to stop her. Please don't go. Please let me talk to you.
My mother pushes him away. Leave me alone, I'm fed up with you.
She slams the door of the elevator shut. We listen to its creaking sound as it makes its way slowly towards the ground floor.
My father meets my gaze and Noga's. Don't bother me, he says.
We nod dutifully and return to our bedrooms.
Noga seems upset and I touch her hand briefly. She'll come back, I say gently. She loves aba.
I know, she says.

A few hours later, my mother reappears. My father embraces her, his arms clasping her small frame.

I lost my temper with your mother, he says, sounding like a guilty child.
I love you, he tells my mother.
I love your mother, he tells us.
It's not enough, my mother answers. You have to respect me, too.

I respect you, of course I do. I'm sorry, he repeats. I have a bad temper. It will never happen again.
You always say that, someone says.
But I can't remember who.

7

In one of the books lining the living-room shelves, there is a reproduction of a Vermeer painting entitled *The Woman With a Water Jug*. She is wearing a cobalt-blue dress. She leans softly towards the jug, while her hand rests on the ledge of an open window.
What is she thinking?
What is her life like?

In that same book, there is a picture of a Memling diptych that hangs in the Metropolitan Museum. The two Portinari portraits.
The patina on the portraits is cracked and I can almost feel it as I run my index finger across the page. Both the man and the woman, who is wearing a beautiful drop necklace around her neck, have their hands clasped in prayer.
They were newlyweds, the accompanying text explains, in small black ink.
Maria Portinari was fourteen years old, her husband Tommaso, an Italian who worked for the Medici bank, was forty-two.
Both of them have a serene expression on their faces. Or so it seems.
How did Maria really feel about marrying a man twenty-eight years her elder?

Will I marry Ilan? Or someone else?
What will I look like when I'm old?
Perhaps I will marry an older man, too.
Or perhaps I won't marry at all.

8

I'm remembering something else, says my father.

We are sitting in the living room. He is leafing through a book while I'm lounging on our velvet, wine-coloured sofa.

Yes?

The day we were deported, I told you my father had his thirty essential oils in his attaché case?

Yes.

Well, after the cattle wagon arrived in Transnistria, we were hauled on to a small boat to cross the Dniester River.

On that boat there were two Gestapo officers, a religious Jew who was clutching his Torah and another man, a very rich banker whom my parents knew from Czernowitz.

This man also held a briefcase in his hand, but his was covered in a cheap cloth. At one point, he opened his case and pulled out a small pot of jam. One of the officers looked at the man and ripped the cheap cloth apart, to reveal a shiny yellow case. He then grabbed the pot of jam and threw it into the river, together with the shiny briefcase. We watched in silence as they sank.

After a while, the man turned towards my father. You see that attaché case they just threw away?

My father nodded.

It was made out of solid gold.

I remain silent. Did you ever see that man again?
No.
That case, it was probably worth a fortune!
Yes, most probably.
Was he walking with you that day? When your father threw you off the slope?
No, I told you. I never saw that man again.
So, what happened after you landed in the forest?
What happened? Simple. My father told us that he had kicked us off because he had found out that we were all being sent to Pechora, a death camp.
But how did he know that?
He knew. He heard it from someone.
And then?
We started walking through the snow. A Romanian soldier appeared and ordered us to stop, pointing his gun at the four of us.
We froze. He said he knew we were Jews. He could tell by looking at us. He asked us what our last wishes were before dying.
That you give us until morning, Pepi answered coolly.

By the time morning came, Pepi knew all there was to know about this soldier. She knew the town he was from, and she knew some of his neighbours. Seeing that he was in the presence of a reputable family, the soldier couldn't bring himself to kill us. So he decided to let us go. He even told us to walk through the swamps so as to avoid the German and Romanian soldiers who were patrolling the forest.
We followed his advice. My father was in pain because of his

wounds, and had trouble walking. We spent the day huddled together in a cemetery. We were wondering what to do next when we found ourselves face to face with a Ukrainian peasant. He had a large moustache and a kind face.

The peasant, who was recently widowed, took us into his hut, in the village of Lucincic, and put us up for three days. He was a good man.

My father pauses. It's important to remember the good men of this world.

We drank vodka with him and spoke about the war. After three days, we decided to go back to the ghetto. There was nowhere else for us to go. The cold was unbearable and my father was in great pain. His wounds hadn't healed.

We arrived back in Luchinetz. By then, there were twenty-five people staying with Mrs Feinstein in the hut, sleeping on pieces of straw.

We lay down on the straw, like all the others. My father with his attaché case, my mother, my sister and myself.

Before falling asleep, my father looked at me and said, *'Sei frei.'* Be free.

And then he died. It was 1 February 1942.

My father looks at me. I mourned him for a long time.

He would have been happy to see what I've become.

9

We spend nine months in London. We live in Kynance Mews, South Kensington. Noga and I attend a French school in Brook Green. I have a teacher there, Mme S, who raps our knuckles with a stick when we misbehave. My grades sink and my parents despair of me.

My sister, however, knows how to use fear to her advantage. She becomes the first in her class in French *orthographe*, an aptitude which will be rewarded years later when she will be selected by a French television channel for the national spelling championship.

My parents see a lot of Kitaj and Sandra, who live in Chelsea. Kitaj is an American painter, as is Sandra, a stunning, dark-haired, blue-eyed beauty. There is something so perfect about her looks and her sweet manner that I detest her straight away.

She's too sweet, I tell my parents.

She's not only sweet and beautiful, she also works hard, says my mother. She's an ambitious woman.

Ambition, according to my father, is a dirty word. *Quelle horreur!* He exclaims, when I ask him about it. If you think about success, *c'est la fin*. The end.

Do you think Sandra is ambitious? Mummy thinks so.

I don't know, he grumbles.

And what about mummy? Don't you think she should be more ambitious? She writes her poetry and hardly anyone ever publishes it.

She must have patience and endure. ENDURE. It will happen.

Do you think it happened to me overnight?
Actually, yes it did, I feel like saying. You always said that success came your way without your doing anything about it.

You were lucky, I manage to say.
Luck? I don't believe in such things.

Whether or not she believes in luck, my mother endures, quietly.
She nurses our aches and pains, and soothes her tempestuous husband.
She cooks and cleans and attempts to restore peace during my screaming matches with my father, or my sister.
Because I scream so loudly that the neighbours complain about me.
When I cross their path, in our building or on the street, I lower my eyes.

Occasionally, my mother finds the time to read and write, in her little study. Sometimes she'll call us in.
Alba, Noga, listen to this, she says.
She reads aloud. Virginia Woolf. Jane Austen. A Shakespeare sonnet. Yeats. Certain words make her eyes suddenly well up with tears, as if she had stumbled on an unexpected stair.

I flee her tears.

My mother falls ill with cancer, recovers, writes a book which does, eventually, get published, but goes unnoticed. She sends out her poems to various magazines. Some get published, many don't. It doesn't seem to matter to her, so why should it to me?

But it does. Her indifference disturbs me. She seems to have given up before even trying. As if she didn't really believe in herself.
What about resilience? About fighting for a cause?

10

Kitaj and my father draw each other's portraits. A bearded Kitaj, a solemn father. They argue about French history and Jewish thought.
Sandra comes over for lunch. My mother serves us smoked salmon. To celebrate, she says.
My father opens a good bottle of white wine. To us! he says, raising his glass.

A few weeks later, Sandra announces that she is expecting a baby and that they're getting married.
They take us to a Texan hamburger place on the Gloucester Road. Kitaj and my father speak about painting and about some friends they now have in common. His enthusiasm for Kitaj has led my father to introduce him to many of his friends. Their enthusiasm for us, however, remains strictly limited. We will not be part of their circle of friends, a glamorous group of painters and writers. Because there is something glamorous about Kitaj and Sandra. I feel it, especially when my parents learn of their wedding, to which they haven't been invited.

My parents are too genuine to be glamorous.
They explain when they should say nothing and react when they should stand back.
All candour, little mystery.
However much they mingle with the aristocracy or the *beau monde* of Parisian society, they are, and always will be, regarded as artists. Slightly eccentric Jewish artists who live in an atelier flat in the 13th arrondissement.

11

Savta fell pregnant again in 1936. She breast-fed her son at the same time as her own mother was breast-feeding her last child.

I can see her, walking across the courtyard of her house, going to visit her mother. She has three children by then, and the older ones cling to her skirt. They ask for food, drink and comfort, and she distributes them evenly.
She is poor, but she doesn't mind. It is all she knows, really. Poverty, child rearing and an enduring belief in God, which keeps her from breaking down on more difficult days.
Sometimes, she needs to remind herself that she has a husband. He is so often away that what he looks like and what she remembers of him have become an indistinct blur.

VII

After Karl died, Pepi and Vigo contracted typhus. So did many others who were sleeping at Mrs Feinstein's.
After a few days, only ten people were left out of the initial twenty-five. The bodies were removed and thrown into a pit.
Pepi fell into a coma. Something had to be done to save her.
My father, who had recovered by then, glanced at Karl's attaché case.
The essential oils. Karl had told him about their various properties.
My father opened the case and started to apply mint on Pepi's heart. He then took some ice from the frozen ground and applied it to her head.
And miraculously, after a few days, Pepi emerged from her coma.

They fled Luchinetz at night. Pepi, Vigo, Elena. They walked for five days and crossed a ravine on a narrow plank. None of them could swim.
They arrived in Mogilev Podolsk. It was a Transnistrian ghetto in German-occupied territory, built by Jews and run by Romanian and German soldiers.

That's when you met that man who protected you? I ask.
Yes. Jagendorf.
I can hear my mother and sister speaking in the kitchen nearby. My mother is preparing dinner. My father gets up, impatiently.

Can't you close the door properly? It stinks! How many times do I have to ask you to close the door? I hate kitchen smells!
He sits back down and grumbles to himself.
Jagendorf? I remind him.
Yes. Siegfried Jagendorf was an important engineer from Bukovina, who had once worked for Siemens. He had made a deal with the authorities, specifically with the governor of Mogilev, to allow him to employ Jewish workers, sparing them extermination.
Jagendorf converted a spare-parts factory into a foundry which rebuilt bridges. He also made stoves for the civilian population and senior government officials.
Between 1941 and 1944, about 10,000 Jews worked for Jagendorf. I was one of them.
We were called his cadets. Our job was to build a bridge over the Dniester River. It was hard work.

He pauses. I remember a little boy, he couldn't have been more than six years old. He sold cigarettes by the bridge. He used to cry out, Zigaretten! Tabak! Zigaretten! Tabak!
The ghetto was very crowded. Ten SS men patrolled the foundry, together with Ukrainian communal guards. They were ruthless.
We were given a bowl of soup a day. A few little lentils floated on the top. We were hungry, always.
People were desperate. They exchanged shoes for a piece of bread. A shirt for a potato. And so on. *Zamekiate,* we called it in Ukrainian. Exchange.
The result was that when the winter of '43 arrived, many people had no shoes left. No clothes.

By January, they were dragging themselves on the ghetto streets like animals, because their legs and feet had frozen.

And your mother and sister? Where were they?
My father stares blankly into space for a long while.
I can't remember, he finally says.

2

The headmistress of the school summons my parents for a meeting. She tells them that I can no longer remain in her establishment. She suggests that they look for another school. Possibly a stricter one would do me good. My grades are poor, my attitude is wrong. All wrong. Too preoccupied with boys, not interested in working. I've skipped many classes and appear to be unruly.

Skipped classes? Preoccupied with boys? Which boys? You're fifteen years old! How could you be kicked out of two schools? And what's this about your attitude? About not being interested in your studies?

I don't care. Or if I do, I'm not sure what it feels like to care.

I won't give you pocket money unless you see a therapist, my mother declares firmly.

My mother books an appointment with a reputable child psychologist on the left bank.

I agree to see him reluctantly.

He is tall, with drooping eyelids, and reclines in his chair when he talks.
What seems to be the problem? he asks me.
Nothing. No problem. My mother told me that if I didn't come here I wouldn't get my pocket money.
I see.
He attempts a smile. And why is your mother so intent on your seeing me?
I've been kicked out of school for the second time.
Why do you think that is? he asks.
I shrug my shoulders. I'm a bad student, I guess.
I see.
He laces his fingers and looks at me intently.
Would you like to tell me more about it?
There's not much to tell . . .
The conversation meanders.
I might be pregnant, I lie.

I'm still a virgin. But no one knows.
Have you consulted a doctor? he asks.
No.
That might be a wise thing to do.
Maybe.

When I return home I tell my mother that I never want to see the therapist again. He was horrible, I say.
I slam my bedroom door shut. I fill my diary with curses about my parents, the headmistress at school and my girlfriends,

Alexandra and Sophie. I play the Clash and the Pretenders on low volume and don't let anyone in until dinner time.

Sam comes over that night. He knocks on my bedroom door. He mentions something about my hair. I've straightened my stubborn curls.
Sam's ethereal presence is soothing. I feel like telling him about the new story I've written.
But I don't dare.
He asks me to play the piano for him. When I am done, he slides on to my piano bench and starts to play a Beethoven sonata.
I turn away. I can identify each note.
I close my eyes. He is playing a C-sharp. Now a D. Now an E-flat.
I hear notes everywhere.
Drops of music that fall like rain into a sea of sound. They are my invisible friends.
I swim in major/minor. I splash in shoals of white keys and startle a timid quaver.
I climb a crescendo, rest on a minim and float away in the arms of a mournful semibreve.
I create the perfect harmony with an A, C and E. Destroy it by introducing a lower black key. C-sharp, for instance.

How easily harmony can sink into discord.

You have perfect pitch, my piano teacher tells me. It's a gift.
A gift? What am I to do with it? Who will benefit from it?
No one except for you, she says.

I now have a weapon. A secret weapon. I'm not sure what to do with it, but that doesn't matter. Knowing it's there makes me feel stronger.

I try partaking in the conversation at dinner.
Sam is talking about the actress Billie Whitelaw and her performance in his play *Not I*.
I speak. My father tells me to be quiet. How many times do I have to ask you not to interrupt? he barks.
Darling, she had something interesting to say, my mother protests. Let her talk.
I look at my sister.
Noga always has something interesting to say. My father never asks her to be quiet.
What did you want to say? my father snaps.
Nothing, I mutter. Nothing interesting.
Not I.

3

One afternoon, after I come back from school, I find my father speaking on the telephone heatedly, relaying what he's hearing to my mother, who is standing by his side, looking very anxious.

Their conversation sounds like a telegram.

Anna.
Fled.

Arab boyfriend.
Disappeared.
It's been six days.
Beirut.
They think.
Yes. Beirut.
Police are on the case.
No.
Not a new boyfriend. Youssef. Family's somehow or other related to Assad in Syria.
Assad!
(A string of invectives ensues.)
Lucia in pieces.
Of course she would be.
. . . Aged ten years in six days.
Of course we will.
Waiter saw them in restaurant.
Champs Elysées.
Champagne? At that age?
Love makes you do crazy things, says my mother.
Yes. Anna is nineteen years old.

(I wish I were nineteen.)

I lose the conversation after that. My father's voice has lowered, as if he has sensed my presence.

I return to my room.
Noga has gone to the cinema with some friends. I wish she were here, so I could tell her about what I've overheard.

Anna has disappeared. Where is she?
What would happen if I were to disappear with a man?
Where would we go?
Would Noga tell on me?

At home, Noga cogitates on the concept of dust while I fret about what shirt to wear.
Her essays are read aloud in school and her gravitas is handled like a precious jewel.
Noga the owl.
I'm cruel towards my sister.
I point my finger at her and snigger.
I choose my words carefully. I search for the most belittling adjectives, just so she can see what I'm capable of.
I am cruel.
I am hard.
I am ruthless.
Indifference is a gleeful revelation. Until guilt makes its surprise appearance, like an oncoming car at a sharp bend.
The collision is crushing.
Noga forgives me.

I close my eyes and try to imagine what it might be like to run away.
I don't think I would have the courage.

I trust you, Anna. In secret. Impetuous Anna.
I wish I could be as free as you are.

4

My piano is my friend. Purchased when I'm fourteen years old, my mahogany Czech upright was once played on by Vladimir Ashkenazy. Or so I'm told.

It is shipped directly into my bedroom and stands against the wall that separates my room from Noga's.

It becomes the recipient of my moods and musical experiments. One afternoon, after having practised a Chopin prelude, I rest my fingers on the keyboard and let them run freely. The result, my first composition, takes me by surprise. No sooner do I try to play it again than I forget it. But instead, another melody miraculously emerges, as if it had been hiding there the whole time.

Notes flying through the air, landing like rambunctious watercolours on the piano.

I can improvise.

I CAN IMPROVISE! I shout.

My mother comes in.

What's all the shouting about? she asks, wiping her hands on a kitchen apron.

I proudly start to play. It's my own composition, I tell her.

That sounds nice, says Noga.

You know what I think about that kind of music, says my father, who has just walked in.

But it's my own composition, I repeat.

There is only one kind of music, he declares, before walking out of the room.

Later I hear my mother reprimand him. Why are you always so discouraging towards her?
When I walk into the kitchen, my father apologises. I'm sorry, he says. He hugs me and kisses the top of my head. Maybe it's good. I don't know about these things.

I know. And this time, I really don't care.

VIII

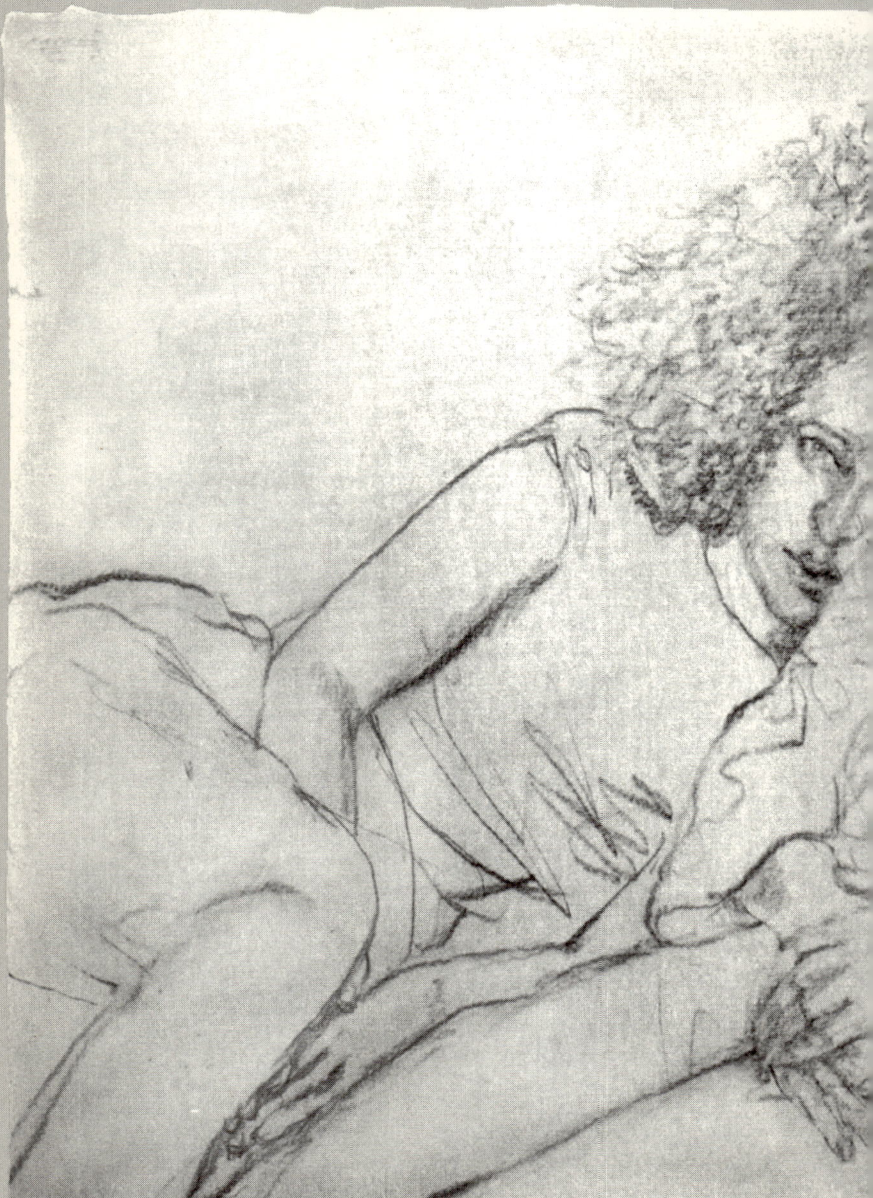

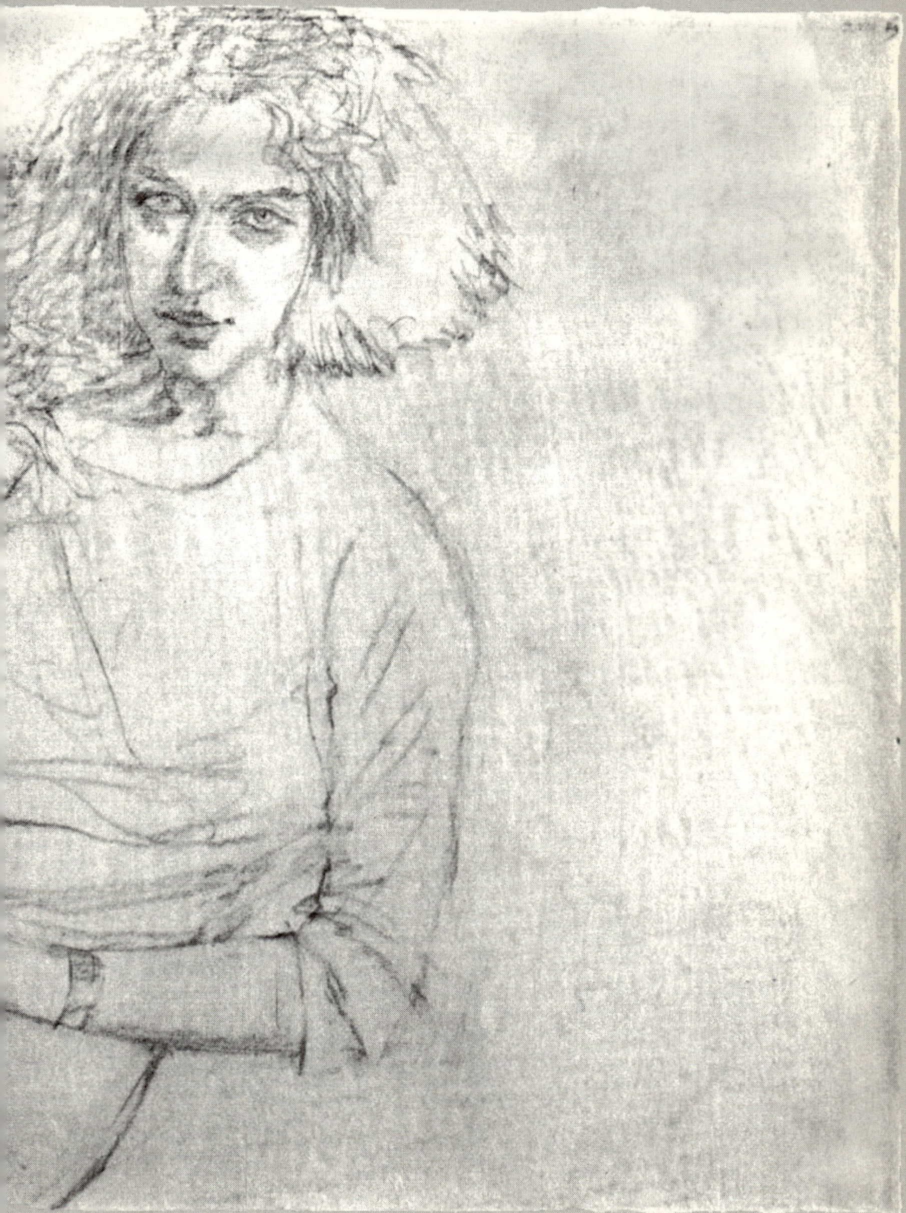

The Marvilles have a sprawling, stone country house in the Oise region, near the small village of Chaumont-en-Vexin. We spend several weekends there, surrounded by various double-barrelled family members of all ages.
Edouard Marville is an ex-prime minister. Slightly hunched and with gentle blue eyes, his towering height seems to shrivel in the presence of his diminutive wife, Jacqueline, a feisty and opinionated woman who addresses her husband in the formal 'vous' and rules over her entourage with intimidating authority.
There is, however, a generous side to Jacqueline. One summer, she offers us a small cottage on their country estate.
Stay there for as long as you like, she says. It's empty.

We stay there for three years running and it becomes 'our country house'. Or, 'our weekend home', as I tell my friends with gleeful pride.

Now, I can finally claim to be one of *them.*
Them, for whom comfort is a priority.
Them, who never speak about money in public because they have it in private.
Them, who haven't read the right books, but are savvier than those who have.

In Chaumont, we befriend a taxi driver who drives us to and from the train station when the need arises.

To and from the supermarket. The pharmacy. The hardware shop.
We become familiar with the region. Meadows and dry hillsides dot the landscape. Noga and I ride our bicycles through the country roads and leap on the haystacks of the next-door farm.
We take walks with my father in the nearby woods. Autumn leaves crackle beneath our feet as he leads the way vigorously through a maze of birch trees.
Breathe!! he cries. He stretches his arms up and down above his head for emphasis. You must breathe in the fresh air!
Noga and I raise our arms up and take in deep breaths. But no matter how hard we try, the fresh air doesn't quite affect us in the same way.

We befriend some of the Marville grandchildren. One of them, Marie, is a year older than me and very tall, like her grandfather. She speaks slowly, as if to make sure that I understand her.

I like Marie but she's a bit weird, I tell my mother.
That's her manner, my mother says. It's the way she pronounces words. Her careful e–nun–ci–a–tion is the way it should be.
Indeed it is. Why can't you speak like Marie? my father interjects. Instead of speaking like all those '68 degenerates . . . What a terrible thing that was, 1968. The beginning of the end. The end of morals and values.

I don't like morals and values, I retort.

One snowy weekend, we light a log fire and sit around the

kitchen table, playing cards. Noga has invited her friend Adam to stay with us.

I have the cards you want, my father announces, midway through the game.

You're not supposed to tell us! we cry out. You're supposed to pretend that you don't have the cards!

So I'm supposed to lie?

It's not a lie, darling, it's a game, my mother says in her soothing voice.

My father throws his cards on the table.

I don't want to play any more, he says. I don't want to lie.

But it's a game! We shriek, in unison.

I don't like games, he announces before getting up and walking away.

2

We fight at home. Loud, terrible fights. I scream and tremble with rage and, sometimes, spit forms on my lips.

My sister retreats to a corner and I throw myself on the floor.

I want to go out. Sophie is having a party. Her parents are away. Olivier will be there.

The boy from the café.

I must go.

Where do you think you're going? What do you think you're doing? I am asked, over and over again. Is this the way a fifteen-year-old behaves?

No, it isn't. But I'm not an ordinary fifteen-year-old and this is not an ordinary family.

My mother takes my side. Tries to explain to my father that I am behaving like a normal adolescent. That there is nothing so terrible about going to Sophie's house.

My father thinks otherwise.

He screams again, I scream back. Please stop it, Noga pleads with us. Please.

Your father was never an adolescent. He doesn't understand what you're going through, my mother tries to explain.

I'm not in a concentration camp! I shout. I have a right to a normal life!

I fall to the floor. This time I have a brief, unconscious spell. When I come to, seconds later, I feel as if I have just returned from a very dark place.

Are you all right? my mother asks.

I don't know, I answer, trembling a little.

Did you faint again?

I don't know . . .

We should ask Dr Bamberger about this, my mother tells my father.

My father acquiesces, shaking his head slowly.

I win the battle. I always do. I know that my father will never punish me all the way. He always stops halfway, a few steps short of enforcing his point.

I'm going, I say, picking myself up, slowly.

You shouldn't wear those high heels, my mother says. They're very pointy. They're going to destroy your feet.

I don't care if they do, I answer. Besides, they're not that pointy.

Be careful, my father says, faltering. Be careful, my darling daughter.
He tries to kiss me goodbye. I push him away.

Be careful. Don't do that. Do this. How dare you? You stupid girl. But beautiful. And talented. But then, how can you waste your talent like you do? And why can't you like the things I do? Why?

Because you like them.

I slam the front door and remove my jeans in the elevator. I take the metro wearing a mini skirt, fishnet stockings, high heels and bright red lipstick. I get off at the Kléber station and walk several blocks to Sophie's house, on the Avenue Kléber. The party is in full swing. The music is loud, several people are dancing. *Pop music talk about. Pop music talk about*, sings a male voice. I join in and throw my arms in the air. I dance until I break into a sweat.
I see Olivier walk towards me.
He wears the same bandanna around his neck. Olivier and I start talking. We smoke a joint. Then, he grabs me and sticks his tongue in my mouth. You're so sexy, he says.

He asks me to dance. I stay in his arms for the rest of the evening. We fondle on a bed in the coat room and he slides his hand underneath my shirt. Then, someone rushes into the room, turns the light on and tells us that the police have arrived.
A few of us leave quickly through the kitchen and out of the

back door. I have a girlfriend, Olivier tells me before I lose sight of him.

Fuck you, I mumble to myself.
I have no money for a taxi and return home on the last metro.
Smudged lipstick. Torn stockings. A large stain on my mini-skirt.
I left my jeans at Sophie's house.
There are two men and a drunken woman sitting across from me.
I am scared.
But I won't show it.

Be careful, my darling daughter.
Yes.

3

My mother's arms are wrapped around me and her perfume envelops me in a cloud of carnation.
Good-night, darling girl. Be nice to your sister, will you?
She switches perfume with the seasons. In winter, l'Heure bleue, Guerlain. In summer, le Dé, Givenchy.
All those scents which blend in with her face creams and make-up. With the warmth of her silky skin.

Many years later, she will fall, hitting her head on the floor of the blue-tiled Auber metro station. Her sense of smell will deteriorate, and she will start mixing perfumes. Chanel with Guerlain. Dior with Givenchy. Sweet and sour, musky and

citrusy. The scents will clash together and I will voice my concern.
I like it, she will argue.
But it doesn't smell good . . .
I like it.

We're going to the Vians, my mother says, that evening. We won't be back too late.

Antoine Vian is the director of the Pompidou Centre; his wife works at the Louvre. They are a good-looking couple and exude the seductive 'Parisianisme' of the Rive Gauche, a slight tinge of bohemianism combined with an irreproachable sophistication.

Am I a true Parisienne? I wonder.
At home, I am a pawn being swirled around various points of the map.
East.
Then further south.
Then somewhere indistinct in the middle.
What middle?
We Jews belong only to our history, my father claims.
No country, then? We don't belong anywhere?
No.
But what about language? Culture? Nationality?
We're Jews, that's all. No nationality.
So there's no such thing as a French Jew? An Italian Jew?
No.
So being Jewish is a culture, then? As well as a religion?
It's a culture and an identity.

Not to me it isn't. Being Jewish is an aside. Like having green eyes. Or curly hair. An intrinsic part of me, perhaps, but not one I pay much attention to. Why would I? It doesn't define me. It only happens to be there.

My thoughts are not prompted by my religion, but by my culture. My French culture, mixed with some Israeli and American roots. Or sympathies. Roots strike me as too intimate a word for these other cultures that, in actuality, feel foreign to me when I visit them, although paradoxically familiar when I'm away.

I speak French with my sister, and occasionally with my father. Outside my home I strive to be a typical Parisienne, unruffled and seemingly self-confident.

At home, we are as far from unruffled as can be. Our mixed ancestry and fiery gene pool make for a heady blend.

Sometimes I want to lay my head on the pillow and pretend I live somewhere else.

But I'm not sure where.

4

We are having dinner. My mother has made us chicken breasts, stuffed tomatoes and spinach.

My father is telling us about the Sumerians.

The Sumerians battled the Akkhadians who migrated to the Arab peninsula and built cities in Mesopotamia. That was in 2080 BC.

Have some spinach, my mother tells me.

No, thank you.
Akkhad was part of the Akkhadian kingdom, my father continues. Alba, stop fidgeting.

I'm not.
There were twelve cities in the kingdom of Sumeria. Do you know what they were?
No.
Darling, how can you expect the girls to know . . . my mother intercedes.
They should! At their age I certainly knew!
The phone rings.
It's a boy, my father says, abruptly handing me the receiver.

I speak quietly. Yes, who is this?
You're a whore, a pubescent voice states. You're a real little whore. Do you know what a whore is, Alba?

Ur. Kish. Lagash.

I hang up, feeling dizzy.

Who was that? my father barks.
I shrug my shoulders, trying to appear nonchalant although my hands are trembling.
Who was it? my father asks again.
I don't know, I mutter. Wrong number.

Sumerian is the oldest writing in the world. Their people were the first to introduce a system of arithmetic. This all happened, as you probably know, during the Ubaid period which was between 6500 and 3800 BC.

I cut my chicken into small pieces, but find that my hands are still trembling, uncontrollably.

5

My back brace is removed. The doctor at the St Vincent de Paul hospital strongly suggests I be operated on.
She needs to have a metal rod inserted in her spine, he tells my mother. Her scoliosis is still very bad. The brace didn't correct it.
We'll think about it, says my mother.

We leave the hospital and I burst into tears. No metal rod, please, I plead. I don't want to be operated on.
My parents eventually relent.
You might be a hunchback when you're older, my mother warns me.
I don't care, I answer.

In the meantime, I live what I am. A young girl, Paris, 1981. Tall and skinny. Long spidery legs and a small waist. Thick, curly hair which I spend hours trying to flatten out.
Lipstick and eyeliner. Croque monsieurs and schnitzels. Hummus and chocolate macaroons. French and English. Mozart sonatas and Serge Gainsbourg. Nightclubs and parties. Cigarettes and torn jeans. Émile Zola and Jack

Kerouac. Degas and de Kooning. Gary Cooper and Alain Delon. Best friends and boyfriends. Seduction and rejection.

At home, I hear all about the new, ignorant generation. About the clash of civilisations. About the old days and the better days and the glorious days of yore.

About how barbarism has invaded our culture. About how everything used to be so much more *raffiné*.
1968 destroyed everything, my father regularly bemoans. When all that barbaric music started with those horrible, vulgar people. Schubert must have turned in his grave . . .

Perhaps. Or perhaps he might have given rock and roll the benefit of the doubt.
After all, the world is filled with talented musicians.
Schubert would have agreed, had he listened to me, not to my father.
He was an open-minded man, Schubert; curious and generous, too.
I can feel it in his music.

6

There was no music in the ghetto of Mogilev Podolsk.
There was the sound of picks and drills, bayonets and rifles.
There was the sound of people crying and people dying.
There was the sound of those executed at night by the Ukrainian communal guards who downed swigs of vodka once they had accomplished their deeds.
There was the sound of bodies being thrown into a pit with a loud thump.
Of men and women being beaten and tortured.
Of children crying and women wiping their tears.
Tss Tss, they'd whisper.
The sound of tentative comfort.
The sound of despair.

We sit in the atelier. A breeze comes in through the open window.

There was a man in the camp called Nauschütz, my father tells me.
Nauschütz was a German officer who had decided to help us.
A very courageous man, he was always accompanied by a dwarf called Max.
Nauschütz dressed Max and looked after him. The latter became an assistant of sorts, and you never saw one without the other. Max the Jewish dwarf, Nauschütz the German officer.
Not long afterwards, Nauschütz showed up with some milk. It had frozen in a metal tin but if one banged hard enough on it, small drops of white liquid would trickle out.

Many got a few drops that day, except for the religious Jews of the ghetto who hated Max. Superstitious and wary of dwarfs, they refused the milk. You bring us bad luck, they'd say. Go away.
Shoo.

Max disappeared and so did Nauschütz.

Did you get to drink any of the milk? I ask my father.
No.
Why not?
I don't remember.
But weren't you starving?
Yes, like everyone else. Many people ate earth, garbage, things they found on the ground. They didn't care. But I did. One day, after my bout of typhus, I found a blue onion buried under the straw. I ate it. I told my mother that this was the best apprenticeship life could offer.
She agreed.
Is that when you started drawing?
Yes. By then, I had been given the status of *Kadett*. I was trained to work with different metal technologies. This enabled Pepi, Elena and me to remain alive. Every three months, eight hundred of us were selected for extermination. Those who were unfit went to their deaths.
Once, during the freezing winter of '43, I dropped a heavy brick I was carrying. It was so cold, I thought my hand had fallen off with the brick.
Saujude! an SS man shouted, slashing me on the back.
I picked up the brick again, wincing with pain. I realised then

how tenuous my position was; I was protected, yes, but for how long?
And what if my mother and sister were sent away instead of me?

One day, a Romanian soldier gave me a tiny pencil and a small sketchbook. That's when I started drawing everything I saw. I painted also, making a paintbrush from my own hair, and mixing pigments in the foundry.
Where are those paintings?
They've disappeared. But you know the drawings.

Yes, I do.

Those drawings depict the corpses of men and women on a cart, children running, beggars knocking on muddy windows, soldiers beating up the beggars, gravediggers' tools. The originals are in the atelier, carefully stacked in a folder.
When my father was reunited with them after the war, he said they smelled of death. Of the camps.
Get rid of them, they stink of death, he told my mother.
She smelled the package.
No smell, she said. Absolutely none.

The phone rings again. A friend of my mother.
I open the kitchen door. I call out and hear my mother pick up the phone.
I sit down again.

Where was I?
The drawings.

Ah, yes.
After I had filled the notebook, I became obsessed with the idea of binding it. I smuggled it into the foundry, under the nose of the SS, and took it to a bookbinder I knew, a man who used to be a friend of my father's. The man bound it for me in colourful paper. White, violet and pink.
I stuck it under my shirt and walked away, my heart beating quickly. Then, an *Arbeits Kommandant* stopped me.
What do we have here? He grabbed the sketchbook from under my shirt and stopped dead in his tracks.
He looked at the drawings, then at me. *Kind, du spielst mit Feuer!* he whispered. You're playing with fire.
He tore off my more explicit drawings and threw them over the ghetto wall. Later, the sketchbook landed in Jagendorf's hands. Only seventeen remained out of the original thirty.
How did you find them again?
My father sighs.
After the war, Jagendorf, who still had the drawings, decided to publish them under one of his children's name.
Pepi was furious and she sued him.
She won, and got the notebook back, via the Israeli ambassador in Bucharest. That's how it found its way to me again.

There is a slight pause in the conversation.
I was angry with my mother, he sighs. I didn't want her to sue him.
He may have been dishonest, Jagendorf, but he saved my life. He saved thousands of lives.
But they were your drawings! I exclaim.
Yes, they were. Yet . . .

Yet what?
It's complicated. Let's have some tea.
All right.
He disappears into the kitchen.

The phone rings. It's Alexandra, my current best friend. She wants to know if I'll go to a party with her on Saturday night. You can sleep over, she says.
Alexandra lives in a modern house in the 15th arrondissement. Her father, a short man with wire-rimmed glasses and an enigmatic smile, is the CEO of a large electronics company. Alexandra's mother is a young and attractive woman who dresses fashionably. She shops and shares clothes with her daughter.
I don't see myself wearing my mother's dresses. Not my size. Too old fashioned.
But her clothes smell good.

My father walks back in, holding a teapot and two cups.
I hang up quickly and return to my seat. He pours the tea, frowning with his bushy eyebrows in the process. Japanese white tea, he says.
I protest. Why can't we drink black tea?
This one's better for you.

Jagendorf promoted me, he says, handing me a cup.
I worked in his office, doing menial duties. After the war, when he was awarded the Order of Lenin by the Soviets, I found out that, while I was working for him, Jagendorf had been busy liaising with Russian partisans in the forest, keeping

them informed of German troop movements, and letting them know when a train would pass by so they could blow it up.
One day, shortly after the Battle of Stalingrad, and after the Russians had gained control of Mogilev, Jagendorf asked me to show a few German officers around the camp. I sat in a car with them as we drove around. A Zinger, it was. I don't think it exists any more.
The Germans looked at me carefully. The child is not Jewish, they decided among themselves. He doesn't have a Jewish nose, nor does he have the ears.

7

When the International Red Cross Commission arrived to inspect the camp, Jagendorf showed them my father's drawings. The men from the commission looked at them in silence.

A few days later, Vigo walked into Jagendorf's office, where he was introduced to two men he had never seen before.
You're leaving today, they told him. Go and fetch your sister.
Vigo's name, together with Elena's, had ended up on a list of fifteen hundred children who were to be evacuated to Palestine, as long as both of their parents were dead.
In order for this evacuation to take place, a deal was struck: in exchange for one million dollars' worth of new trucks, Ion Antonescu, the Romanian prime minister, in tandem with members of the Nazi party, agreed to turn a blind eye. The list of children was supplied by the Red Cross. A Swedish man, a

Jew who lived in Stockholm, instigated the deal.
The man's identity was never fully confirmed.

But Pepi was still alive. So Vigo was given the name of a dead child. Solomon Leder. Same age, similar appearance.
Elena was given the name of a girl, Eva Ackerman.

They said goodbye to Pepi on 4 March 1944. She clasped them against her bosom, tightly, feverishly.
Meine Kinder, meine lieben Kinder, she whispered, tears streaming down her face.

The camp of Mogilev was liberated two weeks after they said goodbye.

IX

My parents call me into the kitchen on a Sunday morning.
We want to tell you something, my mother says.
About Anna, says my father.

I pretend I know nothing.

Anna disappeared with a man, my mother begins.
An Arab, my father interrupts.
She's in Beirut, with this Youssef fellow.
Can you imagine? My father shakes his head in disapproval.
Why did she follow him, stupid girl?
I hope she doesn't stay there for ever, I say, in a broken voice.
I really want to meet her . . .
Meet her? my father looks at me disapprovingly.
She's my cousin.
That's not a reason.

2

Later on that evening, I find out that Anna is coming home.
She has broken up with Youssef who is said to be devastated.

3

My mother announces that Elizabeth is coming for tea. She's

the daughter of a film director, an old friend of the family. Elizabeth is one year older than me, and lives in the 17th arrondissement. Her parents know rock stars and actors and live a glamorous life so far removed from my own, I find it hard to decide whether this meeting will be a good thing or an utter disaster.
Why do you want me to meet this girl? I ask my mother. We have nothing to say to each other.
Why don't you decide after you meet her? she retorts.

When Elizabeth rings the doorbell and appears at our door, I find myself at a loss for words. A blonde-haired young woman with sparkling blue eyes greets me warmly and smiles openly. Her nails are polished and she wears no make-up.
How can one be so effortlessly beautiful?

Do we shake hands? Do we kiss on the cheek? I show her the way to the living room where my father is busy sorting some papers.
Rarely have I felt so self-conscious. So aware of my layers of make-up, my bad skin, my frizzy hair. There is a poise about Elizabeth which I couldn't emulate if I tried; I feel as if I'm speaking with an adult.
How does she do it?
Or am I just particularly immature?

We sit down in the living room. She speaks of school, of her friends, her family.
My parents seem enchanted with her.
What a good influence she could be on Alba, I can almost hear them say.

Before leaving, Elizabeth asks me if I'd like to see an exhibition with her.
Sure, I mutter.

Did you like her? my mother asks, when she finally leaves.
I shrug my shoulders. No, not really, I mumble.
I thought she was lovely, my mother declares.
And beautiful, my father adds. Just like her mother.

We meet a few weeks later and see an exhibition at the Grand Palais.
Elizabeth tells me about her current boyfriend and about the film her mother is shooting. The self-confidence she projects is like a staggering blow. How come everything seems so complicated to me? My identity is tangled like a dreadlock. I wouldn't know how to begin to unravel it.

4

I receive a stamped airmail envelope from Brazil.
I open it feverishly.
A letter from Anna, with a photograph.

Dear Alba,
I've heard so much about you. I really hope we can meet! I'm coming to Paris in late August, and will be finishing my degree at the École du Louvre.
My father said you asked for a photograph of me.
The one I have enclosed was taken in Ipanema, a few months ago. You should really come to Brazil, you'd love it!

I will call your parents when I arrive.
Love,
Anna

She is, indeed, just as I pictured her.
She is sitting on a beach, wearing a short white dress. The sea is in the background. Her body is tanned and fit.
Her hair is dark and wavy and her legs are stretched out in front of her.
There is a gold medallion around her neck.
Her eyes are Korn eyes. Definitely.
A darker version of mine.

I wish I had a gold medallion around my neck.
And tanned legs.
(I never tan.)
And dark, wavy hair.
And a fit body.

I know what I want.
But not what I don't want.
I know who I'd like to be.
But not who I am.

5

In the summer of '82, I see Ilan again, in Jerusalem.
He takes me to a film – *M*, by Fritz Lang.
Our knees briefly touch before the end. Afterwards, we go to a

restaurant overlooking Mount Zion. We eat quiches and he does most of the talking.
After dinner, we climb into his car and go for a drive. We stop off at various points, and he shows me the hills and the stars. The Mount of Olives and the town of Silwan, in the distance. He puts his arms around me and I can feel myself weaken at the knees.
You've become a very pretty young woman, he tells me.
I am tongue-tied.

Later on, he kisses me in front of my house. It was nice to see you again, he says, before climbing back into his car.
I'll call you, he adds, before driving away.

6

We visit Elena and her husband Ezechiel on Jaffa Street, in Jerusalem.
Ezechiel, a photographer, works for the Jewish Agency. He sits in a corner fiddling with a camera.
Elena fusses around us. She is overweight and smokes heavily. She wears thick glasses and has sweaty armpits.

Elena has let herself go, my mother says. She used to be attractive.
How does one let oneself go? Is it triggered by unhappiness or the humdrumness of a union?
A friend of my mother's often refers to her husband as 'my better half'.

I cannot think of anything worse than becoming someone else's other half.

I want to talk to Elena alone. Find out more about Eva Ackerman, and what happened on the train when they left for Palestine.
I'm too shy to ask. So my father does it for me.
Alba wants to know the Eva story, he tells her.
Elena looks at me. Come see me alone and I'll tell you everything you want to know.
I'm glad you have a curious daughter, she tells my father.
She's sixteen, my father groans.
Remember when we were sixteen?
My father nods quietly and says something to her in German. Their own private history.
I return to Elena's apartment the following day.
She offers me tea and cake, just like Pepi.
She pants when she walks, and a few drops of sweat trickle from her temples.
She grabs a pink box of pills on a side table, swallows a few quickly, and looks at me.
I'm not in the best of health, she tells me. My heart, she adds, pointing towards her large bosom. You're lucky you're young and pretty. My daughter, Tamar, she's pretty too. But you don't know her well. You could have been friends the two of you.
Yes, I mumble, feeling my cheeks redden.
Elena looks at me. It's OK, you have a difficult father, it's not your fault. He's been like that ever since he was a child.
She smiles at me and I smile back politely.

You have a whole future in front of you. I no longer do. But that's fine. I've lived the life I chose.

Is this really the life you chose? I wonder.

I look at Elena.
Her apartment is sad. Her husband is sad. She is ill.
Does one choose one's life?
Perhaps it fans into place serendipitously, like a hand of cards. One pick, one path, with a few shuffles in between.

Elena interrupts my thoughts.
You're not here to listen to my rants and raves. You're here because of Eva Ackerman. Is that right?
Yes.
OK. So lower the shade, please, there's too much sun, and pour us some peach tea.

I pour the cold tea into two blue glasses.
Your father was my parents' favourite, she begins by telling me. He was the talented one. The intelligent one.

I'm not sure what to say. I don't particularly want to hear her diatribes against my father.

Your father is not an easy man, she repeats, smiling. But he's very talented. So we try to forgive him.
We both laugh.
You know that I saved his life, do you?
I nod. Yes. I know.
And yet, he's always angry with me . . .

He's not angry.
Oh yes he is, she says in a strained voice. He's very angry.
Do you want to know what happened the day I saved his life?

No, I don't. I only want to hear about Eva.
But I can't tell her that.

I think I know the story, I mumble instead.
No, you don't. You know your father's version. Not mine.
Elena became a nurse after they arrived in Israel.
They settled in Ma'ale Ha-hamisha.
In January 1948, right before the Israeli War of Independence, a local Arab army ambushed my father's convoy. He was shot in his left lung and between two vertebrae in his back. He was eighteen at the time.
He sank into a coma and was quickly pronounced dead. He was moved to the hospital mortuary with a label bearing his name tied to his body.
A nurse who knew Elena ran to get her. Your brother's been shot dead, she told her. They're about to lower him into the grave.
Elena rushed to the scene. She saw my father's thumb move imperceptibly and was able to get him to an operating table where a surgeon agreed to perform a second operation.

I saw the light, my father once told me. After I was shot, I felt myself being squeezed out of a tight space and propelled into the sky. I saw my body far beneath me. I was in excruciating pain. I came to and blanked out several times.
At one point, I found myself in an ambulance, surrounded by journalists.

I lapsed once more into a coma and woke up eight days later, in hospital.
Every four hours, I was given morphine. After a month, I was dismissed and sent back to the front line, covered in bandages.

I saw my grave, carved in rock.
It remained there for several years before it was finally destroyed.
I was too young to understand the meaning of it.
I still don't understand it.

7

The cattle wagon that left Mogilev Podolsk on 4 March 1944 was covered with red crosses, like a tapestry. It smelled of filth and urine, but none of them cared; it was a small price to pay for their freedom.
Of all the fifteen hundred children who boarded, between the ages of five and twenty, only Vigo and Elena had false identities.

They were briefed before leaving. They were now Eva and Solomon. Nineteen and fifteen years old, respectively. The Moldavian border town of Braila was filled with SS officers. There would be an interrogation.

Eva and Solomon.
Eva and Solomon.
Eva and Solomon.

Right before boarding, a man who worked at the foundry took Elena aside. There's been some confusion, he said, with some hesitation in his voice.
What is it?
Eva Ackerman is alive. She'll be on the train with you.
Elena felt the colour drain from her face.
What should I do?
Nothing, the man answered. She's been given the name of Miriam Shinsky. It will be fine, don't worry.

But Elena did worry.

The wagon left. None of the children spoke. Many slept, some cried. One boy told another that he had dreamt for the first time in two years.

Then, twenty-four hours before the border, a young boy they knew came up to Vigo and Elena, speaking breathlessly.

Eva doesn't want you to use her name, he told them. She's been crying the whole time about it. I know what's going on, Eva told me everything. Because of the two of you, we're all going to die.
Where's Eva? Elena asked, in a trembling voice. I want to speak to her.

She squeezed her way through the crowd of children. By then, the secret had travelled throughout the car. There were two illegal children on board, and all their lives were at risk.

Someone pointed out Eva to Elena. Even in the half-shadow she could distinguish her features. Large eyes, thick eyebrows, sharp cheekbones; she looked older than her nineteen years. Her head was resting against the filthy wall and she clasped her hands tightly. She wasn't crying any more but her voice trembled when she spoke.

My name is all I have left, Eva said. My parents are dead. My sister is dead. My two brothers are dead. I'm not giving my name up and I don't want you to use it.

Elena swallowed hard. It's just until the border, that's all. After that you can be Eva again . . . I understand how hard this is for you, but – and here her voice faltered – but if you don't do it, we could all die. At least my brother and I certainly will.

I won't give up my name and you are not to use it, Eva repeated, in a high-pitched voice.
She crossed her arms defiantly and turned her face towards the crowd of children who had gathered around her.
I've got nothing else to lose, she added, her voice dropping suddenly.

A young man who was standing next to her put his arm round her shoulders. That's not true, he said in a soothing voice. You have your whole life to live! You're going to the promised land! Everything will change for you, for all of us!

But Eva wouldn't hear of it. She remained seated, her head against the wall.
Elena began to cry softly, covering her face with her hands.

Vigo, who had been quiet until then, went up to her. Please don't cry, he said. Don't. Let me speak to her.
He walked over to Eva and crouched by her side.
Eva, he said in as firm a voice as he could muster, all of us have lost our families on this train, which is why we're together.
But you didn't! She cried out. You still have family! You're frauds, the two of you!!
A few other voices rose in unison. Frauds! You're frauds!

You must do what the man in the ghetto said, Vigo continued, ignoring what was happening around him. Please let my sister use your name. Just until the border. After that, it will never be spoken of again.

Eva shook her head resolutely.
No, she said. I'm not doing it.

In that case, we're all going to die, Vigo announced gravely.

A few hours before the border, the mood started to change. A few older children gathered around Eva. Come on, Eva, you'll get your name back! All you have to do is answer 'Hier' when they call out Miriam. You can do it! We know you can do it!
Eva shook her head. You don't understand. None of you understands.
At that point, it was indeed Eva whom they didn't understand. But they said nothing.
By then Elena had stopped talking.
There was nothing left to say.

In Braila, the SS made them all get off the train. They rounded them up and called their names alphabetically. When it came to Ackerman, Elena shouted, Hier! Her eyes gazing steadily in front of her.

When it came to Shinsky there was a long silence, and the SS officer got impatient. *Also? Was passiert? Wo ist Miriam Shinsky?* The silence lingered in the air and all eyes were riveted on Eva. After what seemed like an eternity, she finally answered, in a barely audible voice.

Hier.

The SS officer grumbled something and ordered them to get back on the train. When Vigo went to look for Elena, he found her beaming, her hands clutching Eva's, who didn't respond. Her eyes were fixed on the large red crosses on the wall.

I'll never forget you, Elena murmured, before letting go of her hands.

They arrived at the port of Constanta, in Romania. They were divided into several groups.
Vigo and Elena boarded a ship bearing the Red Cross flag.
They marvelled at the expanse of blue sea.
Oranges floated in the water, like balloons.

They had forgotten what fruit looked like.

They saw Eva board a smaller ship and set sail for Istanbul, just like them.

Then they lost sight of her.

Out of those fifteen hundred children, only a hundred and thirty made it to shore. The other boats were blown up by mines on the way to Palestine.

8

Elena takes a sip of her tea and looks at me.
The story doesn't end in Istanbul, she says.

Her voice sounds raspy and breathless.

You can tell me another time.
No. I'll tell you now. Give me a cigarette, will you? There's a pack over there, on the kitchen table.
I hesitate.

Go! She bellows.

I return with a crumpled pack of Parliaments.
Elena lights one and turns her head towards the window.
It's a hot day today, she declares. I'm glad we're inside.
I nod.

She turns round and flicks her ash in an ashtray.

I moved to Jerusalem, married Ezechiel and became a school nurse. I worked mostly in kindergartens.

One day, thirty years later, an Orthodox woman wearing a beige kerchief around her head came to talk to me about her little boy. She had concerns about the fact that Oded didn't interact with his classmates. He comes home crying every day, she said.

Is he ill? Is something wrong?

As she was talking, the woman kept staring at me in a peculiar way, which made me uncomfortable. I realised it was the woman's eyes. I had seen them somewhere before, but I couldn't remember where.

I gave the woman advice as to how to handle her child, and the conversation was left at that.

But a week later the woman came back, saying she saw no improvement in her child. As she talked, I experienced the same feeling, as if I had seen her somewhere before. I offered further advice, and as the woman walked away, she suddenly turned round and looked at me hesitantly.

Is there something else? I asked.

The woman shook her head and walked away.

Two weeks passed and she came back again. This time, I didn't know what to say. Oded appeared to be in fine health, and I didn't think he looked unhappy at school: he seemed to get along perfectly well with the other children.

The woman lowered her eyes to the ground, then raised them again.

Mrs May, she said, in a trembling voice. You don't know anything about me, but I know everything about you. I'm not here for my son. He's fine. I'm here because I've been tracking you down for over thirty years. I know where you live, whom you married, what you called your children. I know what synagogue you go to, where you buy your bread, where you get your hair done. I've known you since you were a young girl, standing in that cattle wagon with your brother . . .

I looked at her. The large eyes, the thick eyebrows, the sharp cheekbones.
Eva Ackerman.

I felt dizzy. I reached for a nearby table, dropping a few coloured pencils in the process.

I'm sorry for what I did to you, all those years ago, Eva said. I've tried to say it before and . . . I couldn't.
It's fine, I answered, trying to control the tremor in my voice. We're both here now, alive and well.
Yes, we are, Eva murmured.
I'm sorry, she repeated.

Eva left quietly, closing the door behind her.
I knelt down and picked up the pencils, one by one.

I never saw Eva or Oded after that day. When I enquired about their whereabouts, I was told that the family had moved to a settlement, near the Lebanese border.

X

I call Ilan. He tells me that he's very busy.
I'll call you in a few days, he promises.
He won't call me. I know it.
I burst into tears after hanging up the phone.
Does he know how I feel about him?
I've never loved before.
It hurts.

2

The curtains in Savta's apartment are made of cheap white lace. The view from her windows is of Chicoun Habbad, drab 1950s' buildings which house a large proportion of the Orthodox community.
We take the bus to Savta's with my mother, who always seems a little jittery before we get there.
Do they get along? They take each other for granted, mother and daughter, with a tacit acknowledgement, rather than understanding, of their respective lives.

As a free-spirited child, my mother had often wondered whether her parents were really her own. How else to explain her love of books? Her curiosity about the world? How come she was so different from her parents?
So my mother read books in secret; her parents wouldn't have approved.

Stories about jilted lovers and conquered lands. Victorian and Edwardian novels where love and luck win out.
This was the world she belonged to.
At seventeen years old, my mother broke free. She left home and never returned.
The bitterness between Savta and her eventually gave way to a modicum of civility.
My mother had married, after all. And she had children.

When my mother's first book of poems was published, Savta held the book in her hands.
Her own daughter's book.
She couldn't read the words inside.
So she kissed the cover.

3

Savta squashes her nose against our cheeks, kissing us repeatedly when she sees us. Her lips are wet.
How are you? she asks, several times.
Well. We're well. And you, Savta, how are you?
She throws her arms up in the air. I'm fine, *vat* can I do . . . ?
We sit around Savta's table. Stuffed cabbage and coleslaw, schnitzel and cheese blintzes.
Have you met a nice young man? Savta asks me, with a twinkle in her eye.
She's sixteen, my mother tells her.
So? I was married at seventeen.

I have a boyfriend, I tell Savta, as Noga looks at me disapprovingly.
You always have boyfriends . . .
Shut up, I hiss.
Is he Jewish? Savta asks.
He's called Matthieu and he's a punk, Noga tells Savta.
A *vat*?
Never mind, I mutter. Anyway, he's not my boyfriend any more, I snap, turning towards Noga. Pierre is my boyfriend, not Matthieu.
(This isn't quite true. I like Pierre, but he doesn't know it.)

Savta wipes the corner of her mouth with a paper napkin. Next boy, she declares, will be a nice Jewish boy. Maybe even a husband, *baruch' ha shem.*
She's sixteen, my mother reiterates.
Soon she'll be seventeen, Savta quips.

I think of Pierre. He's very tall, with dark hair and green eyes. Women swoon over him and speak about him in giggly whispers.
We smoked a joint together at a party, a month ago. I wore a tight, white blouse with a mini skirt and high-heeled pumps. I drew a black line of kohl over my eyelids and painted my lips a bright red.

Where are you going, looking like this? My father asked, lifting his head up from the book he was reading.
Looking like what?

You know exactly what.
To a party, I answered, before running out of the door and slamming it shut behind me.
The party was on the Rue de la Pompe, in the 16th arrondissement. A large, sprawling flat with imposing paintings and Persian carpets in every room. Two waiters, dressed in white, were serving drinks behind a bar.
Cecile, our host, was dressed in a see-through black dress. Her long, blonde hair spilled over her shoulders with studied nonchalance. Diamond earrings shone in her lobes. Men looked at Cecile because she was beautiful. She spoke with a slow, deep voice and when she laughed, her teeth sparkled.
At one point during the party, Pierre arrived. He kissed me on both cheeks. When he saw Cecile, he put his arm around her waist and I felt a sting of jealousy.

Pierre and I danced to Elvis Costello and Rita Mitsouko. Our hands touched a few times. The tips of his fingers felt warm.
Sophie came towards us and started dancing next to me. Pierre's really cute, she said, a little too loudly.
I didn't answer. Sophie seemed drunk and wobbled a bit as she danced. She had cut her hair short and wore too much make-up.
After the party, as a group of us walked back towards the Trocadero metro station, Pierre asked me for my phone number. Sophie pulled me aside and cupped her hand over my ear. I could smell alcohol on her breath.
Don't give it to him, she whispered. Let him wait.
Why? I asked. I like him.
Let him run after you, she replied. He'll like you even more.

Pierre didn't ask for my number again and ran after Sophie instead.
I haven't spoken to her since. Nor do I intend to.

Have some more schnitzel, it's good for a growing girl, Savta says.
I'm already grown-up, I reply.

4

After the camp of Mogilev was liberated, Pepi was caught between the advancing Russian army and the retreating Germans.
She fled from the Ukraine to Romania, a bullet lodged in her leg.
She walked hundreds of kilometers until she reached the capital, where she was cared for by her surviving brother.
She settled in Bucharest. Many days were spent at the Red Cross office, where she, like hundreds of others, searched desperately for news of her children.

Were they alive?
There were alarming reports of boats being blown up by mines before they made it to Palestine.
Of trains stopped and searched before the border.

There were sleepless days and nights, thinking the worst.
Dead.
Alive.
Dead.

Alive.
No.
Yes.

And then one day, a letter.
They were alive, in Jerusalem.

It would be fourteen years before Communist Romania would allow Pepi to leave the country and be reunited with her family.

Those years needed to be filled.
Quickly.

She chose to become a beautician. She had a special touch.
Good hands, too.
Slender, pale fingers which didn't betray her darker past.
The grime, the slime, the putridity around her.
She had smelled and touched death, like all the others.
Yet, Pepi's hands had been spared.

She chose to lose herself in the world of creams and potions, make-up and gels. She found that it was an efficient way of shutting out the painful memory of her children.

I can see her.
Her soft, grey curls. Her brown eyes, broken mirrors of pain.
Her smile. Cautious.
Just in case.

She shuffles about her salon, mixing potions with various ingredients.
Beeswax. Lanolin. Cocoa butter. Almond oil.

She applies them carefully. In a circular motion around cheekbones and foreheads, cheeks and chins, eyelids and temples.
Soon, her reputation grows.
These creams are lovely, Frau Feldman. What is your secret?

Because by then Pepi has met and married Jean Feldman, a Romanian photographer.
They settle in a small apartment.
I imagine it, small and stuffy. They argue about draughts.
We need some air, Jean tells Pepi. It smells in here.
I'm cold, Pepi answers.

You're always cold, Jean sighs.

Pepi cooks for Jean. Recipes from Czernowitz. Black-bean soup and *Shelinsuppe.* Schnitzel and potato pancakes.
Sometimes they go out for dinner.
More often than not they stay at home.

I can see Pepi walking to her salon in the morning. She wears her dainty pearl earrings and red lipstick. She carries a leather handbag and sometimes, when it's sunny, wears a straw hat. She has gained a little weight around the hips and stomach. She doesn't love Jean the way she loved Karl. But that doesn't matter, really. Being alive is more than she expected.

She walks slowly, her thoughts carrying her beyond the streets of Bucharest, across the Mediterranean to where her children live.

Soon, she will join them.
Soon.

5

In 1957, Pepi was allowed out of Bucharest with only one small suitcase of belongings.
She boarded a train to Vienna.
She arrived on the platform and looked for Vigo.
He had trouble finding her at first.
Then, a frailer and shorter woman than he remembered called out his name.
Vigo!
Her cry, as shrill as the train whistle.
He ran towards her and she held him tight against her bosom.
Tightly. Warmly. Strongly.
She handed him a cooked chicken she had placed in a plastic bag.
For you, she said.

The next day, Vigo took her to a concert at the Musikverein.
She couldn't concentrate on the music. It was too much to bear.

Later, in a restaurant, he told her all about his life. He was living in Paris. He had become a famous painter. He had made friends with people she had never heard of. Giacometti, Beckett, Raymond Queneau.

He wasn't married, but had girlfriends, here and there.
In Israel he had become something of a legend. He had friends in high places.
I'm going back to Paris, but I'll come and visit you in Jerusalem,

he said. I wrote to the President, who's a friend of mine. He'll be sure you're well taken care of.

She found herself a flat in Jerusalem.
Jean was able to join her the following year.
She opened a beauty salon, just like she had in Bucharest.

But sadness never really left Pepi's side. It had become part of her, like a frayed hem on a piece of clothing.

Jean died. Soon, Pepi became ill and needed proper care.
Elena chose to put her in a nursing home in Haifa, one which Pepi's brother Dori had built. We visited her there a few times.
She wore the same brown-and-white-polka-dot dress and cried when she saw us.
Always.

XI

My mother and father met in 1959. My mother had heard about him through a friend of hers, Gershon, a philosopher who taught at Trinity College, Dublin.
The man's a bit strange and without a telephone, Gershon told her. But you should write to him and tell him you'll be passing through Paris. You might get along.

She explained that she had just arrived from New York, where she had completed her graduate degree at Sarah-Lawrence College. She was on her way to Jerusalem, but would be in Paris for a few days, where she was sharing a hotel room with her friend Marcia.

I immediately liked her handwriting, my father said. I guessed that she was a poet by the shape of her letters. And when I met her, I liked everything about her.

They met at the Café Cluny on the Boulevard St Germain. It was a warm June day.
My mother wore a royal-blue dress with a bright emerald-green belt and matching blue shoes. She arrived a bit late, having gone to the hairdresser, who had wrapped her thick, black hair into a bun.

She didn't need to scan the room in order to find my father; she spotted him instantly. Wiry hair, round-rim glasses, smoking unfiltered cigarettes. He seemed nervous and jittery when she approached his table.

His English was basic, but they managed to communicate nevertheless.
If you were to name the most important things to you, what would they be? my father asked her.

Music, the Bible and poetry, my mother answered, after a slight pause.

And art? What about art?
Yes, yes, art. Of course.

She knew much less about art than she let on. Would he hold it against her?
The conversation switched to poetry. He recited a Rilke poem in German.
She recited a psalm in Hebrew.
You speak Hebrew with an American accent, he said.
You don't like it, do you?
No, he answered, his blue eyes boring into hers.

There was nothing she could do about it. Her accent was moulded by her past:
Her mother and father.
Her teachers in Brooklyn.
The streets of Manhattan.

The present defined my father's life. He dismissed his past with a wave of his hand when she asked him about it.
Let's not talk about our families, he said. Let's recite more poetry instead.
They did.

Later on that evening, they went to Lipp's, a brasserie on the Boulevard St Germain.
My father knew many of the people who were sitting on the terrace.

He introduced my mother. Anne, from New York.
She shook many hands and smiled mechanically. A few people asked her questions, which she couldn't understand.
I don't speak French, she said, shyly.

This was an important meeting, she later told Marcia.
You should stay in Paris, Marcia suggested. Get to know him better.

My mother moved into a *chambre de bonne* on the Boulevard Malesherbes, in the 17th arrondissement.
There was no bathroom there, so she took to using the washrooms of the American Express office, on the nearby Avenue de l'Opera.

During the day she taught English at the Berlitz Institute.

In the evening she saw my father.

And after a few months she moved into his atelier, Villa d'Alesia, in the 14th arrondissement.

She spoke no French. She couldn't cook and could barely get around the city.
When my father went out in the evenings, she stayed at home. She wasn't ready for the *beau monde* Parisien which he frequented at that time. Friends with famous names and famous faces, who spoke in torrential French and tentative English.

I can picture my mother, book in hand, curled up on the sofa at the Villa d'Alesia, waiting for my father to come home.
She was often alone.
But she didn't mind.
Or so she said.

She began taking French classes at the Alliance Française.
Slowly, she learnt the language and was able to immerse herself in my father's life.
It was a far cry from the world she knew.

They married in 1961, in Manhattan.
A religious wedding attended by my mother's family.
My father didn't invite any of his friends.

Too many differences to reckon with.

2

Anna calls.
She's in Paris, living with her new boyfriend, a film producer.
Let's meet, she says.
I can hardly wait.
Place St Sulpice, four o'clock. The café by the church.
I change my clothes three times before settling on a pair of tight jeans, my cowboy boots and a shirt which hides the acne bumps on my chest. I apply foundation that conceals the pimples on my face.
Never mind the fact that the foundation is much darker than my neckline.
Or the fact that I wear such heavy mascara on my eyes that it sticks the lashes together like glue.

I jump on the no. 83 bus.
I sit in front of a man who eyes me suspiciously. I turn my face away, focusing on the Rue d'Assas and the hordes of students who stand smoking on the sidewalk.
As I'm about to get off the bus the man asks me if I've ever done any modelling.
I laugh. Model? Me? No. Not at all.
You should think about it, he says. I'm a photographer for *Jardin des Modes*, a fashion magazine. Do you know it?
I do.
But I pretend otherwise.
Bad habit of mine.

He hands me a card. Give me a call, he says. After you've discussed this with your parents, he adds.

Fashion model.
Fashion model!

I run to the Place St Sulpice. I sit at the Café de la Mairie and pull out a cigarette.
I wait for Anna.
I smoke, one cigarette after another.

She never comes.
I fiddle with the fashion photographer's card. Then, I crumple it into an ashtray, stand up quickly and walk away.

3

I shut myself in my bedroom for three days, with the novel *Belle du Seigneur*, Albert Cohen's thousand-page magnum opus. Set in Geneva, it is a love story between Ariane and Solal, a beautiful couple whose passion, set against the backdrop of the war, eventually ends in tragedy.

My mother calls me in for dinner.
I'm not hungry, I say. I'm in the middle of the most important part.
You haven't eaten lunch . . .
Later, mummy, later.

I am gripped. I am Ariane and Solal is Ilan.

I plunge into their world. 1936 Geneva. Their villa, their bed, their thoughts, their touch.
I lick the words with my tongue and feel them melting on my palate.
I crave to be them.
I crave to know them.
My reality is transposed to their surroundings.
I stand before them, an invisible witness to their fervid passion.

4

I start going out with Pierre. He is no longer with Sophie, who is said to be heartbroken.
But I don't care.

Pierre lives in the 16th arrondissement with his mother and younger brother.
Whenever his mother is away, Pierre throws parties. Large parties filled with bohemian types, high-school friends and strangers.
We roll joints and drink screwdrivers. We dance until early morning, our bodies glued to each other. At dawn, we drive to the Place des Abbesses and buy croissants from a local bakery. We eat them, standing by the Sacré Coeur, Paris sprawled beneath our feet while a pink sun rises slowly before us.

At Pierre's last party, an American man takes my hand and reads my palm. He seems perplexed. You have no lifeline, he says.
What does that mean?
I'm not sure. Could be good. Could also be bad.

To this day, I wonder.

5

My grades are better. But the atmosphere at home isn't.
My father shouts.
I shout back.
He screams.
I scream back.

There are no boundaries at home. Neither on his side, nor mine.

That summer, Pierre invites me to his summer house in the Corrèze region. A large house with a swimming pool and a garden. A uniformed maid serves us our meals.
Bourgeois heaven.
I feel happy, away from my family. We sleep in separate bedrooms and Pierre sneaks into my room at night. We kiss and fondle, but I don't let him go all the way.
Not yet.
I'll wait, he says. But not for long.

One afternoon, the phone rings.
It's your father, Pierre's mother tells me.
I sigh. God, not him, I tell Pierre.
I pick up the phone rudely.
What is it? I snap.
His voice sounds different. Lower. Slower.
My mother died this morning, he says. She'll be buried in Jerusalem.
He hangs up the phone abruptly.

I clutch the receiver in my hand for a long time.
I'm sorry, I whisper.

I hear a dog bark in the distance. Voices clamouring for me next door.
À table! Le dejeuner est servi!
Sounds of plates and cutlery. A woman laughs melodiously.
Pierre's mother.

Alba ist ein schönes Mädchen . . .
Pepi in her polka-dot dress.
The nursing home on the hilltops of Haifa.
She smiles at me. A beaming, tender smile.
She is seated in a rocking chair.
Back and forth.
Back.
And forth.

6

I have decided to leave home.
I will be spending my last year of high school with a family in America. They are related to an elderly friend of my mother's, in Manhattan.
It is a rash solution, but one which seems sound at the time.
I will write.
I will call.
I will try to become a better person.
I am young, still. Seventeen years old.
Young and angry.

Time to go.

7

Dear Anna,
We never got to meet each other because you don't exist.
You are a figment of my imagination, my exotic contrary.
A projected glimpse of normality in my life.
I thought that by imagining you, I might become a little bit like you.
That my supposed association with you might render me more interesting in the eyes of those who didn't find me so.
But this has not happened.
My family will never be normal. I will never be you.
No fabrication will change me.
Life will.

Maybe someone like you does exist, somewhere in the world. I hope they do. I liked you.

Goodbye, my imaginary cousin.

I've never met Josi, or his wife. They live in Brazil, but none of us knows where. Pepi did mention São Paulo, once. But even she had lost contact with the Korns.

The fantasy of Anna is being replaced by a steadier reality, which is progressively taking hold of my life. Imagination is becoming less of an escape, more of a creative need.

Just like my father.
And my mother.

8

Noga cries when I leave.
I don't want to live here without you, she says.
My mother cries too.
My father looks distraught.
I swallow hard and keep my tears to myself.
Too late to backtrack.

Must go on.

ILLUSTRATIONS

Page 10, *Anne in profile*, 1973, by Avigdor Arikha.
Sugar lift aquatint on handmade rag paper © Trustees of the British Museum.

Page 78, *Mirror with self-portrait and press*, 1971, self portrait by Avigdor Arikha.
Etching © estate of the artist.

Page 154, *Alba and Noga*, 1989. Soft graphite on Japan laid paper © estate of the artist.